W9-BRY-048

Praise for

MICHAEL BERNARD BECKWITH'S

# SPIRITUAL LIBERATION

"For a spiritual reference, this one book would be sufficient for a lifetime. It connects with one's spirit directly in an activating mode that enhances one's spiritual endeavor. It is definitely a 4-star must read that is not only erudite, but eloquent and inspirationally elegant in its content and style."

—**David R. Hawkins**, MD, PhD, author of *Power vs. Force*

"Even in the midst of technology-based modernity, the voice of the indigenous spirit is not lost; these pages invite us to listen to the ancient wisdom residing in the deep waters of our psyches."

—**Malidoma Patrice Somé**, PhD,
author of *Healing Wisdom of Africa*

"I have known Michael Beckwith for seventeen years. I have never witnessed anyone who walks the talk as much as he does. His words and actions have been an inspiration to me and have changed my life more than I ever envisioned."

—**Mark R. Harris**, producer of the movie *Crash*,
winner of three Academy Award

"Michael Beckwith's inspiring book is a testimony to the potential of us all to become a Buddha. This book will help others to reach inner freedom for the sake of all sentient beings and world peace."

—**Talhun Khen Rinpoche Geshe Kachen Lobzang Tsetan**,
abbot of Tashi Lhunpo Monastery in exile, Bylakuppe, India

"With this book, Michael Beckwith shows us once again that he is a true innovator—a teacher who leads us all toward the global spiritual evolution of our planet, by opening us to greater depths and understanding of ourselves and the world."

—**Pete Carroll**, head football coach,
University of Southern California

"Michael Bernard Beckwith's message is the emerging conversation for our culture. His eloquence in articulating the nearly unspeakable experience of awakening to our true essence brings a practical note to the increasingly chaotic symphony at play in our time."

—**Dr. Sue Morter**, founder of Morter Health Center

"Every experience Michael recounts is an instantaneous kindling of intuitive, spiritual awakening in us. He almost involuntarily takes our lives completely to a luminous, transformative touch. Michael breaks through all the barriers created by the followers of Great Ones and compounds us into one shared spiritual consciousness. It is not just another book to be read—in every sentence you feel the transformative energy process."

—**Dr. A. T. Ariyaratne**,
founder of Sarvodaya Shramadana Movement, Sri Lanka

"Michael Bernard Beckwith is a leading teacher of a non-exclusive spirituality, a mature cosmology and metaphysics. He takes us to a level of insight on spiritual development seldom achieved. With exceptional clarity and poetic power he sets down the stages and steps in spiritual awareness and growth."

—**Lawrence E. Carter**, dean of Morehouse College
and author of *Ethical Global Options*

"Throughout this book, Beckwith gently challenges us to live courageously, authentically, and to make the most out of our glorious earthly sojourn. His message changes lives."

—**Hill Harper**, actor

"Michael Beckwith's words will inspire and drive you to change your life for the better, enhancing your spiritual practices in a way that's inclusive, not elitist."

—**Elton Brand**, Philadelphia 76ers

"More than informational or inspirational, although Michael Beckwith is both, this man's message is truly transformational. This book will change your life in every important way."

—**Mary Manin Morrissey**, author of *No Less Than Greatness*

"Michael's teachings are a blessing and have inspired our whole family. We are so pleased that his love, wisdom, and consciousness can be shared with everyone."

—**Catherine Oxenberg** and **Casper Van Dien**, actors

# SPIRITUAL LIBERATION

## FULFILLING YOUR SOUL'S POTENTIAL

MICHAEL BERNARD BECKWITH

**ATRIA** BOOKS
New York London Toronto Sydney

Hillsboro, Oregon

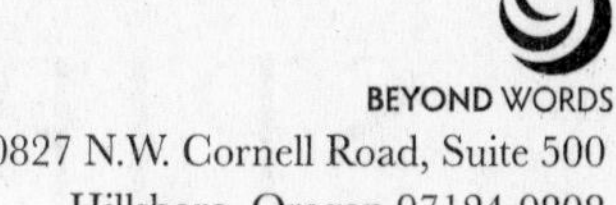

ATRIA BOOKS
A Division of Simon & Schuster, Inc.
1230 Avenue of the Americas
New York, NY 10020

BEYOND WORDS
20827 N.W. Cornell Road, Suite 500
Hillsboro, Oregon 97124-9808

Copyright © 2008 by Michael Bernard Beckwith

All rights reserved, including the right to reproduce this book or portions thereof in any form whatsoever without the prior written permission of Atria Books/Beyond Words Publishing, Inc., except where permitted by law.

*The Holy Bible, New King James Version*, Copyright © 1982 by Thomas Nelson, Inc.
*The New King James Bible, New Testament*, Copyright © 1979 by Thomas Nelson, Inc.
*The New King James Bible, New Testament and Psalms*, Copyright © 1980 by Thomas Nelson, Inc.

Epigrams used at the beginning of each book chapter are published and copyrighted by Eternal Dance Music, all rights reserved. *I Found a Deeper Love* © 2003, *In the Land of I Am* © 2000, *From Within* © 2003, *I Walk in the Love of God* © 1996

Managing editor: Lindsay S. Brown
Editor: Anita Rehker, Adrienne Ingrum
Copyeditor: Henry Covey
Proofreader: Marvin Moore
Interior Design: Devon Smith
Composition: William H. Brunson Typography Services

**ATRIA** BOOKS and colophon are trademarks of Simon & Schuster, Inc.
Beyond Words Publishing is a division of Simon & Schuster, Inc.

Manufactured in the United States of America

ISBN-13: 978-1-58270-199-8

The corporate mission of Beyond Words Publishing, Inc.: *Inspire to Integrity*

*This book is dedicated to the love and musical sound scape of my life, Rickie Byars Beckwith, my wife; to my parents, Alice and Francis Beckwith, for their example of goodness of heart; and to my children, Kiilu and Micaela, whom I love beyond words.*

Colors, like numbers, have their own vibrational qualities. Springing from nature itself, color has its origin in a higher reality. Blue represents the formless substance of the Christ Consciousness pervading all creation. The field of the mystical third eye is blue. Since antiquity, blue has been used by the world's spiritual traditions in its iconography to represent a high state of spiritual awakening. Mary's robe is depicted as blue; Krishna's skin is blue; Buddha is blue; Islamic tiles have the same hue of deep blue as Christian stained glass windows. Blue has been chosen as the ink color for the pages of this book because of its equivalence with that which is mystical, so that the vibration of the Christ Consciousness may be roused in the reader's heart and soul.

# Contents

# Foreword

I have known Michael Bernard Beckwith for quite a few years. I have heard him speak many times; I have spoken at his spiritual community, Agape International Spiritual Center; I have attended his services; I have traveled on the same international expeditions and been at the same domestic conferences; I have personally discussed God and love and politics with him, and we have sat down together for the occasional meal.

In every single one of those situations, I have always met the same Michael. There is something stalwart, strong, and consistent about him. He takes life very seriously but himself not at all. And I have never heard him say anything that suggested in the slightest that his spiritual convictions were not for real.

Now, I have encountered him again, as will you, on the pages of this book. The man, the minister, the sage, the philosopher, pours much of what he has learned from his years of study and experience into this heartfelt treatise on what it means to be a human being deeply connected to our spiritual roots, becoming free of our worldly delusions, and rising up to our divine potential. I believe him on the pages of this book as I believe him in personal relationship, for the same man comes through in print as comes through in his sermons and in his friendship. In reading this book, you will encounter more than spiritual information; you will encounter a soulful man with a wonderful mind who has both honed his intellect and opened his heart, studied abstract theology, and embraced the suffering among us. Over the years I have known him, Michael has become a thought leader and a spiritual teacher. This book is a climactic articulation of what he has learned, what he has taught, and what he has become.

His journey has been a very human one, and the richness of the man is part of the richness of his teaching. Michael Bernard Beckwith, through his ever-deepening understanding of God and human existence, has already cast a wide net of influence. With this book, the many lessons he has learned, the information he has accumulated, and the insights that have illumined his mind will now illumine yours. The riches this book holds for you are like the richness of the man himself. You will be blessed by both.

Marianne Williamson

# Acknowledgments

So many steps of my journey were foretold to me in the lucid dream state, beginning with my great-grandfather, Reverend Arthur Chichester, founder of St. Luke's Baptist Church in Washington, D.C. When he appeared to me, in addition to announcing that I had overcome the hereditary tendency of the Chichester boys to "go crazy," he added this prophetic remark: "Welcome to your life of service." I deeply appreciate his ethereal tap on my shoulder, which sensitized me to my life's calling. I gratefully acknowledge the loving support of my ancestors, my brothers Akili and Tony, and my entire family.

Some years later, I had a lucid dream of being in a large auditorium where Dr. Homer Johnson and Dr. Dan Morgan were presiding on the dais delivering a spiritual discourse. Dr. Johnson motioned to me to join them and asked that I read a Bible passage to the congregation. As I did so, individuals became deeply affected, and some even started to cry as spontaneous healings began to occur. I was so stunned by this that I stopped reading in mid-sentence. My two mentors each whispered in my ear words that indicated my life would follow in their footsteps. An inner transformation began that continues to this day, for which I profoundly thank them.

Soon thereafter I began a practice of leaving my workplace and driving to the beach. Once there, I climbed to a remote area that became my personal "power spot"—a collection of enormous boulders from which I had a view very much like the background on this book jacket. During these times, I had a recurring lucid dream where I was magnetically drawn toward a large building out of whose windows a joyous crescendo of sound spilled out onto the street. Once inside, I saw people of all ethic stripes harmoniously celebrating existence. Although my presence was invisible to them, a familiar inner voice said, "This is what you are to do." It seemed incredulous, and all I managed to meekly respond each time was, "How?" to which the reply was, "When you surrender, the rest will unfold." Today I can say that this atmosphere greatly resembles that of the Agape International Spiritual Center, which I founded in 1986.

Many other dream-revelations have since taken tangible form, including one that occurred during an African pilgrimage in the late 1990s. In the dream state, a dark-haired woman visited me. We didn't speak, but I understood that she was to play a significant role in my work. Just months later, at a faculty meeting, I noticed a volunteer working in the office across the hall. To my surprise, it was the woman in my dream. I excused myself from the meeting, approached her, and looking her straight in the eye asked, "What are you really doing here?" Shyly but clearly she replied, "I've come to edit your writings." To Anita Rehker, my editor, thank you for your commitment to your spiritual practices which powerfully come through in your work, and for your dedication to bringing my teachings to the world in written form. I have noticed, with respect and appreciation, your unconditional loyalty to presenting them just as they have evolved throughout the ten years of our working together.

I thank my beautiful friends at Beyond Words Publishing—Richard Cohn, Cynthia Black, Lindsay Brown, and Courtney Dunham, all of them I consider family and with whom it has been a special joy to work and play. My gratitude to Judith Curr and Malaika Adero of Atria Books, and to Adrienne Ingrum, developmental editor of my book—their expertise and support have been invaluable.

I want to acknowledge all those who supported me during Agape's founding twenty-two years ago: Reverends Joan Steadman, Nirvana Reginald Gayle, Coco Stewart, Deborah Johnson, and Eunice Chalfant. To Reverend Carol Traylor and Patti Ballard, who receive these words in the next dimension of life, I thank you for our eternal friendship. I thank all past and present members of Agape's Board of Trustees for their contribution.

I thank Agape's staff ministers Leon Campbell, Joanne Coleman, John Elliott, Daytra Hansel, Dr. Maisha Hazzard, Dr. Audrey Levy, Safire Rose, Greta Shesheta, and Andrea Waters for your unconditional commitment to the Agape Movement.

I profoundly thank Reverend Cheryl Ward, dean of Agape's University of Transformational Studies and Leadership, and a long-time member of Agape's board of trustees, who has so selflessly given of her gifts, talents, and skills. To the thousands of students who have matriculated through UTSLA over the years, thank you.

I profoundly thank Kathleen McNamara, director of Agape's Practitioner Core, who, along with Agape's licensed practitioners, has lovingly held this book in prayer.

To Lissa Sprinkles, who "knew me when . . . ," I thank you for your prayers, love, and spiritual friendship. To all of Agape's dedicated staff–you are the lifeblood of our vision and mission, and I thank you from my heart for the gift of your consciousness. I profusely thank Agape's ministry and department heads and the hundreds of sacred service personnel for your commitment to being a beneficial presence on the planet. To the members of the Agape International Choir, your voices amplify the beauty of the Universal One. And finally, I thank the thousands of members of the Agape community who have loved and supported me unconditionally and whose graciousness allows me to fulfill my soul's potential.

May all of these supporting energies continue to let the Light shine forth.

# Introduction

The book you hold in your hands is not just another self-help book telling you how to get more of what you think you need to be happy and anti-bored until you die. Its purpose is to stir you up, to ignite within you a desire to establish a transformative spiritual practice, and to show how to cultivate and sustain that spiritual practice. The spiritual strategies described in this book will shift your dependence on the outer things of life to make you happy to rely on your own inner authority as a fully empowered being.

Our inner Spirit is the most vibrantly real and ecstatic aspect of our being. It's puzzling that we have to be educated in how to spiritually awaken, how to activate our soul-potential, especially when considering that enlightenment is inherent within us. It's not a matter for philosophy, however, because the roots of our intellect do not reach deeply enough into our spiritual marrow to contact the source and purpose of our existence. Spiritual awakening is a journey of the heart. Every person's heart is aflame to know its true nature, to commune with its Source. Lao-Tzu put it beautifully when he urged his students to "Use the light that dwells within you to regain your natural clarity of sight." And yet, few of us even know that this inner light exists, let alone that we may access and apply it to our spiritual, mental, emotional, creative, or physical life structures. The good news is that for those of us who yearn for it like a drowning man craves breath, spiritual practices are available so that we may realize our "natural clarity of sight" to which Lao-tzu refers.

This book addresses some of the most fundamental questions about the process of waking up. What is the nature of this Great Something we call God and what is our relationship to it? What are the laws governing the universe and how may we apply them in the mystical and earthy matters of life? What does it mean to become enlightened? What are the marks of a spiritually evolved person? How may we cultivate our talents and skills and creatively, meaningfully express them? Do we actually influence the planet and individuals who live across the world?

Today's consciousness research and quantum physics reveal that consciousness interpenetrates all that is, affirming that existence is not random, that it is intentional and governed by universal law. To that I add love. We are governed by law and love. There is no absolute definition of God or Love. They are synonymously indefinable. However, we intrinsically know when we experience a burst of realization or sense a presence that can only be called God or Love. Neither is visible, nor can they be analyzed by the thinking mind or intellect. They can only be realized. Although I use such words as Source, Love-Beauty, Presence, Ineffable, and Spirit to represent the Godhead, none of them is adequate to describe the Great Something we call God that is everywhere in its fullness.

# Introduction

*Spiritual Liberation* is not the result of my having reached ultimate spiritual conclusions that I now present as being "*the* truth." It is rather a summation of my own journey of some thirty years of entering the Great Mystery and exploring frontiers of consciousness, which is an ever-evolving process. It is the result of my having discarded a materialistic worldview and replaced it with the realization that a committed spiritual practice illuminates and clarifies our purpose on the planet. We are freed not only by what happens when we sit on our meditation cushion but also by how we apply the results of our spiritual practices when driving on the freeway or interacting with others, nature and the global environment, how we cultivate our world citizenry in relationship to our brothers and sisters on the planet, how we compassionately extend ourselves in selfless service and share our resources.

In the first chapter of this book, "Love-Beauty," my accent is on the beginnings of my spiritual opening, which I hope will provide readers a basis for understanding "where I'm coming from." The next six chapters describe my core teachings. Beginning with the seventh chapter and throughout the rest of the book, I offer practical tools that are applicable to spiritual aspirants at all levels of practice.

At the end of each chapter, I have included an affirmation that grounds the principles covered in the text, as well as an "embodiment" that you may wish to include during your meditation, prayer, or contemplative times.

There are terms I use when teaching for which, for clarity's sake, definitions follow. Heaven, for example, is not a location. We are in heaven when we live in an inner realization of the ever-expanding good that exists throughout the cosmos.

The fundamental goodness of the universe is a description of the fact that we live in a friendly universe that has been intentionally designed to foster our awakening. It is not against us; it is for us. It does not test us; it cheers us on. Our Authentic Self is our inherently enlightened state, what the Buddhists call our original face and Christians define as soul.

Transformation is a much-overused word in today's spiritual vernacular. So often it's used as a promotional mantra intended to hook the prospective seminar attendee, reader, or magazine subscriber. In this book, transformation is that which occurs when identification with the egoic self is superceded by a conscious realization of the Authentic Self. There are two kinds of warriors in the world: the traditional warrior, who protects borders and a way of life, and a spiritual warrior. A spiritual warrior breaks through inner borders and discovers new dimensions of an expanded way of being. A spiritual warrior is an individual who is fully committed to their spiritual awakening and is courageous enough to make choices based on this commitment. My use of the word surrender represents our inner willingness to let go into the next stage of our evolution. Just recently I coined the word "playvolving," which means to remain in a high inner state of play while simultaneously being aware that you are here to evolve in consciousness.

Some chapters contain brief references to the Life Visioning Process, or simply visioning, which is a spiritual practice I originated when founding the Agape International Spiritual Center. Because practice of the Life Visioning Process is quite detailed in nature, I have not described it in this book. You may, however, learn more about it from my six-CD set, *The Life Visioning Process.*

The epigraphs that appear at the head of each chapter are lyrics taken from the songs that my wife, Rickie Byars Beckwith, and I have written over the last twenty years. Their purpose is to convey the tenor of the subject matter within the chapter.

# Introduction

This book not only conveys a message *to* you, it will also elicit *from* you insights into your own true nature and purpose. Your existence as a unique and precious being is deeply and enduringly known by your inner Self. It is my conviction that we have not only the capacity but also the mandate to consciously participate in an evolutionary process that introduces us to the Authentic Self. My part has been to design a guide that you may use to enter this deeper dimension of being.

An enlightened society can only be created by awakened beings. It is my fervent prayer that you will be inspired to reveal your innate capacity to become a beneficial presence on the planet and actively contribute peace, compassion, lovingkindness, and selfless service to humanity and our world.

# 1
# Love-Beauty

*A surge of life pulled me from the dead*
*I gave up mental contamination*
*And started building a spiritual foundation*
*The world all around me was falling down*
*And when it crumbled I saw higher ground*
*Something happened inside of me*
*I stepped into my true identity*

My central message is not about religiosity or churchianity. It is about aspiring toward spiritual liberation, which I define as becoming free from the narrow confines of fear, doubt, worry, and lack, and living instead from a conscious awareness of one's Authentic Self, one's true nature of wholeness.

Spiritual liberation results from discovering and expressing the intrinsic qualities of enlightened consciousness that have been ours since the moment we came into existence. Simply put, all that is required to live up to our highest potential is already inside us awaiting our conscious activation. Living up to our potential is about becoming more ourselves, more of who and what we are as awakened beings, a central theme you will encounter throughout this book.

Growing into spiritual adulthood has to do with understanding that we are here to attune ourselves to the evolutionary impulse that governs the universe, which is infinite, conscious, and seeks to articulate itself by means of us. We live in a universe where nothing remains static. All that exists has an observable impulsion to become more fully itself. An acorn seed, when planted in good soil and provided the proper nutrients, ultimately evolves into its fullest potential as an oak tree. Likewise, in order to fully evolve, the Spirit-seed at the core of our being must be cultivated. We too must till the soil of our consciousness with spiritual tools and inner nutrients that enable us to fully deliver our gifts, talents, and skills. Through this inner work, our consciousness becomes a fertile condition for our *conscious* participation in our evolution, rather than a natural selection process driven by external conditions.

Jesus the Christ, Gautama the Buddha, Bhagavan Krishna, and many others are examples of spiritually liberated beings. They are our way showers. *Each of them provides a unique map leading to the same destination, whether it's defined as self-realization, enlightenment, satori, nirvana, perfect sanity, samadhi, or ecstasy*. We, like them, are candidates for awakening. In fact, we have a mandate to wake up to our true nature and the nature of Reality.

## ALIGNMENT WITH UNIVERSAL LAWS

As we spiritually mature, we discover that there are universal laws that can be used to accelerate our evolution. In the beginning stages, these laws are applied to get our legitimate needs met. For example, prosperity is a livelihood focus; healing the body is a health focus; and a relationship is a love focus. By aligning ourselves with the laws that govern these aspects of our humanity, our life structures stabilize and we are free to move into deeper dimensions of our being. With our energies no longer entirely focused on feeding, clothing, and housing, we are free to enter the real work to discover and release what the poet Robert Browning called our "inner splendor."

# Spiritual Liberation

## MY ENTRY INTO THE SPIRITUAL LIFE

Social activism and making a constructive difference in the world were focal points in the Los Angeles household of my childhood. My parents' generosity of heart and community values were strong influences on me and my two brothers. Their example contributed to my involvement in anti-Vietnam protests during high school, boycotting businesses that paid unfair wages to people of color, and my membership in the Black Worker's Congress and the establishment of the Harriet Tubman Prison Committee in college. I enthusiastically participated in these and other socially acceptable activities of the '60s and '70s. I was known to be an agnostic, so my unorthodox spiritual opening came as much of a surprise to my family and friends as it did to me.

In the early 1970s I was a student at the University of Southern California, majoring in psychobiology, a time when smoking marijuana was, well, the norm. What I was learning in classes about mental illness caused me to wonder if echoes of some childhood experiences wherein I experienced visions were pathological. I cut back on the marijuana, hoping the visions and voices would stop. Instead, they only intensified.

To cover the expense of my recreational use, I began selling marijuana. What started as a modest cottage industry ended up with distribution in D.C., Atlanta, Nashville, New York, and Los Angeles.

Then something happened that made it impossible for me to keep turning my back on my inner experiences or attributing them solely to smoking weed. For about a year, I'd been having a recurring dream of being chased by three men. I'd always wake up before they actually grabbed me, but each time I had the dream, they got closer and closer. Then, one night, they caught me. I struggled against my dream captors. Out of the corner of my eye, I saw a small tent with hundreds of people I knew standing in line to get in. I shouted to them for help. They looked in my direction, but one by one they turned their backs to me. Suddenly, two of the men pinned me down while the third plunged a knife into my heart. The pain was excruciating. I screamed out, and then I died.

When I awoke from this dream-death, I felt myself interpenetrated and surrounded by a magnificent presence. Because I had agnostic leanings, I identified it as Love-Beauty. It pierced my spirit with unconditional love, the same love that enlivened everything in my immediate surroundings. The person who had spent so many years denying his connection to the Universal One had died; I could never fit into that box again. I began studying both Eastern and Western spirituality and mysticism. I found that when you stripped away the culture, history, and dogma of every religion, the teachers of those religions were teaching very similar principles and practices that led to a sense of oneness, that ended a sense of separation from the Whole.

Encouraged by this discovery, my desire to use and sell marijuana died. I decided to quit and get out of the business—but not before arranging to sell the delivery I had just received. Never before had I stored marijuana in my home. But, for this final sale, I made an exception. Before I could distribute it, I got busted, compliments of an informant, by the police.

The size of my operation made the charges serious. I faced significant jail time. Well-meaning friends gave me advice ranging from "plea bargain" to "take your money and get out of the country." But to my mind, none of it was relevant because the person who'd been the drug dealer was dead—my spiritual transformation had made me a new individual—and I intuitively knew, beyond all doubt, that the new me wasn't headed for jail.

Day after day, I sat in the courtroom reading spiritual books until a moment when, out of the blue, my lawyer leapt up and convincingly made a point about a technicality. The judge then requested a meeting with the attorneys in his chambers that resulted in a three-day recess. When I returned to court on the fourth day, my case was dismissed.

The judge, however, had his own words of wisdom for me. After dismissing the charges, he called me to the bench and sternly admonished, "That was a lucky break, young man. I hope I *never* see you in my courtroom again."

I looked him straight in the eye and responded, "And you never will." Right there, on that courtroom floor, I vowed to myself: From this moment forward my life is dedicated to serving Love-Beauty in the world.

Relieved to be outside the confines of the courtroom, I took long, deep breaths as I drove home, my heart overflowing with gratitude. As I got out of my car and began walking toward the front door, my attention was magnetically drawn to a weathervane in my neighbor's front yard. The afternoon breeze had a velocity just strong enough to blow the point of the weathervane away from me. Riveted on the weathervane, I mentally commanded, "If my inner experience is really about all that I believe it to be, then let the weathervane turn in my direction . . . " Before I could even finish my sentence, the weathervane turned and stopped with the arrow pointing right at me. Love-Beauty pierced me at my core. I surrendered my life completely to its luminous, transforming touch. I realized that my outer life was now aligning with the inner transformation that had begun with the recurring dream a year earlier. No more signs were required!

I dove into spiritual inquiry through meditation, contemplation, prayer, retreats, pilgrimages, and the study of Eastern and

Western mysticism, metaphysics, and science. I experienced the profound joy of consciously communing with the Love-Beauty that enlivens the universe and in that communion realized a radical sense of my own aliveness. I consecrated my life to this Love-Beauty, trusting its goodness to guide the course of my life. I learned that I was not special because of my experiences, that all of us do eventually awaken to an awareness of being much more than flesh, bone, and mind.

### ABANDON SPIRITUAL SHYNESS

Many individuals have had intimations of an inner awakening, and many have indeed become fully self-realized. Perhaps you have not dared to share your own aloud, thinking, as I did, that they border on the pathological or that you would not be believed. I hope that by openly describing my journey, you will be encouraged to not dismiss or discard the revelations and insights that have knocked at the door of your awareness. If you have mentally packed them away, bring them out into the light and revisit them. Trust them. Stir them to life again and allow yourself to be led into further openings of consciousness. And, if and when it feels appropriate to do so, share them. You never know when your path will be the impetus for another individual to seek his or her own unique relationship with the Ineffable. I'm an advocate of setting aside self-consciousness and being vulnerable enough to look foolish for the love of the Spirit.

### MYSTICS TRANSCEND THEOLOGY

What a blessing it has been throughout these some thirty years now to have studied with individuals of enlightened awareness—those who are still living and those who are not. Theirs was not mere conjecture or blind faith. They had conscious, ecstatic awareness of a tangible Presence. They were genuine vehicles who contributed to the awakening of their disciples, devotees, students, and even individuals who resisted their influence. How fortunate we are that their spiritual realizations and insights were documented in their autobiographies and other writings, biographies, and books written by their students and devotees.

I carry in my heart a profound gratitude to my teachers of the East including Sri Aurobindo, Paramahansa Yogananda, Guatama Buddha, Krishnamurti, and Osho. The Sufi mystic Hazrat Inayat Khan and his teachings came into my life at just the right time. The life and teachings of Jesus the Christ have always had a major impact on my life. My Western influences include Dr. Ernest Holmes, George Washington Carver, Dr. Thomas Hora, Emanuel Swedenborg, Pierre Teilhard de Chardin, Walter Russell, Joel Goldsmith, Dr. Howard Thurman, and Thomas R. Kelly. Others influenced my spiritual growth, but I remain in humble gratitude to these earlier spiritual guides by whose legacies I have been so deeply graced and inspired.

From my studies of scriptural texts and mystical writings of East and West, it became clear that they are not at odds. Their writers and teachers emphasized different aspects of the awakening process depending upon their time in human history and their respective audiences. The closer you get to the heart of their messages there is less contradiction. The world's spiritual traditions have produced many mystics, and in their writings and poetry all dogma disappears and religious titles and creeds dissolve. Only the taste of the Infinite remains on their lips and speaks through their writings. They stand in agreement that there is a dynamic Presence that is the life force enlivening all that there is, that which longs to articulate itself through all beings, and for that purpose has empowered us with the capacity to co-create our lives in harmony with the laws governing the universe. This natural expression of our innate wholeness is enlightenment.

Fortunately for us, generous individuals who were successful in outwitting the limitations of language have shared their process for arriving at self-realization. Once we grasp the urgency of wasting no more time and applying what they have gifted us, we too will know the joy and peace of mind and heart that come from waking up. It is then that we'll come into the fullness of our spiritual inheritance as innately enlightened beings. Studying the lives and teachings of the great ones and practicing their teachings, we too will awaken to the realization that we are and always have been spiritual beings having a human incarnation. From that platform, we become a beneficial presence on the planet and individual expressions of humanity's next level of evolution.

### Affirmation

*Right here and right now, I call forth and activate the evolutionary impulse of my inner being. With absolute trust, I surrender to where the Spirit leads me and experience the peace that surpasseth all understanding.*

Take a relaxing breath and contemplate the following embodiment.

### Embodiment

I turn within at this moment, feeling the joy of simply being alive—joy that I can give thanks for something, regardless of what it is. Thank you divine presence. Thank you pure Spirit. I turn within during this moment and feel your presence. I recognize it everywhere. Everywhere I am, you are. I am becoming so unified with your presence that I hear you saying to me, "I am closer than your breathing, nearer than your hands and feet. The very ground that you're standing on is holy."

I feel it now, and into this zone of feeling I enter, knowing that a spiritual quickening is already taking place within me.

When Jesus defined prayer, he said to pray believing that I already have so that I may receive. He didn't say pray believing that I *might* have it or pray believing that it *will* happen at some future time. No! So I now pray believing that heaven is already where I live. Ever-expanding good is already mine. I claim it as my spiritual inheritance. So I now enter into a zone where I realize that all of my needs are met. I feel that, right now, regardless of my circumstances. No one is preventing me from feeling that I already have all of my needs met. There's no outside authority saying, "You know you can't feel that yet because you don't have the money you want and you don't live in the house you want to live in. No, you can't feel that yet." I *do* feel it now, I feel and believe I have all I need, right now. Abundance is the order of the day. No longer do I have anxious thoughts about how my needs will be met.

I speak this word for myself knowing that in the feeling tone of this vibration my life contains all beauty, all love, all wisdom, all peace, all supply, all joy. Life so flows through my entire being without inhibition that the magnetic field within me magnifies the living Spirit in such a way that I ride a tidal wave of its beauty. This is what I'm declaring. This is what I see. This is what I accept. This is what I know. It's happening now.

Into this sacred "now" I speak. I call forth wholeness and well-being in my life. My body temple reflects the fundamental harmony of the universe—the order, the strength, the beauty, the revitalizing power. Oh, the way I am made! So marvelously made! Divine Intelligence within my body temple can heal anything as I allow the condition for healing to manifest. So I say "yes" to every organ, action, and function of my body. I am made whole. Every cell now vibrates with a luminosity that comes with having an intimate at-one-ment with pure Spirit. Health is the order of my day. Wholeness reigns supreme.

My mental habits and patterns are now refined, are now restored to their original clarity, and I no longer count my failures and obstacles. I count my blessings. As I go through my day, I am grateful. I start counting, "Oh I'm so glad I've got a table. I'm so glad I've got a floor. I'm so glad I've got a rug." I just count my blessings. It doesn't matter how big or small they are. I'm totally grateful.

My body temple, my emotional body, my mental body, the body of my affairs, my relationships, my creativity, all are now congruent with the fundamental goodness and harmony of the universe. I see and I give thanks for this. How infinite and divine and perfect is the spirit that indwells me. I give great thanks for the truth that pulses through me in this moment, allowing me to have direct contact with the fullness of my being.

I know that this word I speak is a law of elimination that dissolves anything that previously hindered, blocked, delayed, obstructed, or denied the fullness of life from expressing in and through me. This word is a law unto that which has been spoken. It is now the very condition that allows the divine and perfect spiritual idea within me to evolve into full bloom. I see it even as I declare it. I know it. I walk in a trust atmosphere about it. It governs my steps. It lifts me up. It transmutes anything within me that would hinder or block me. I open and am receptive to the inflow of inspiration, expansion of consciousness, and revelation of my true nature as an awakened being in this very moment. It is done, and so I let it be.

# 2
# Evolved People

*Make me patient when I worry*
*Make me calm where there is strife*
*Make me loving when my heart is hard*
*Make me forgiving when I would be right*

Patterns of thought and action develop over the course of a lifetime. Some of these patterns support us while others undermine us. They impact our quality of life and interactions with our world. Upon examining our everyday patterns, if we are honest, we will notice how, beginning with our morning routine until the time we go to sleep, we consistently use one muscle: repetition. Sleep on one side of the bed long enough and it becomes "my side." Even if there is no one sleeping in your bed but you, it's still "my side."

Once we become conscious of the patterns we have formed, we can revisit them and make new choices where we feel necessary, or as a practice to keep ourselves flexible, or simply to consciously exercise our power of choice.

Just as we have been given the power to create patterns of thought and action, so do we have the power to change them. Choosing which ones we want to continue and the ones we want to change or drop is an exercise in freedom. It comes down to understanding that we have been given dominion over our lives as described in the Bible, "To him was given dominion and glory . . . his dominion is an everlasting dominion."[1] We are, each of us, kings and queens sitting on the throne of consciousness ruling our lives. *When we have dominion over our thoughts and actions, we experience freedom from the bondage of mechanical living.* Dominion moves us into a space of being that characterizes practices of evolved people.

Reality has dominion over illusion. You have been created to have dominion over your illusory, impermanent thought forms. To the degree that you exercise that dominion, you will experience what Jesus the Christ meant when he encouraged us to "Consider the lilies of the field, how they grow; they neither toil nor spin, yet I tell you, even Solomon in all his glory was not clothed like one of these. But if God so clothed the grass of the field . . . will he not much more clothe you?"[2] As you move into embodying dominion, you become confident that the plentitude, health, love, and creativity that are your spiritual birthrights will blossom into your life and adorn you, just as the lilies of the field experience all their needs being met.

### THE ROLES OF INVOLUTION AND EVOLUTION

Involution is the prototype inherent within someone or something. Evolution is a by-product of involution. A maple tree seed is involute; it already carries the prototype of the tree. Nothing needs to be added, subtracted, or changed *within the seed itself* to prepare it to sprout. Evolution is the seed becoming more of itself over time. Similarly, human beings exist as a perfect prototype in Universal Mind. There is absolutely nothing missing within us; we have been equipped with everything we need to evolve and flourish. Just as a seed needs the proper soil, water, and nutrients to grow into its perfect expression, so are we to nourish the soil of our consciousness in order to evolve into our soul's ever-expanding potential. Integrating the spiritual principle of involution and evolution enables us to move through the world with dominion as we flex the inner muscle of choice—rather than repetition—where our thoughts and actions are concerned.

Embracing the seven practices that follow will support you in uprooting thought forms and habit patterns that sabotage your spiritual progress.

## EVOLVED PEOPLE GIVE THANKS FOR WHAT MOST PEOPLE ORDINARILY TAKE FOR GRANTED

Evolved people give thanks for life, for the intelligence within the body temple, within nature, for what most people don't even notice as they navigate through their day. Gratitude is an expression of humility, a recognition that even before we ask, good has been given to us.

Gratitude also includes respect for what the ego would call "bad news," the challenging circumstances that come into our life to wake us up. Individuals who are unaware of the sacredness of all expressions of existence live their lives against a backdrop of complaining, self-pity, and excuses. They are busy directing their energy toward changing the things and people around them, rather than themselves.

About two years ago, in one of Agape's University of Transformational Studies and Leadership (UTSLA) classes, I invited students to present any requests they had for prayer. Donna, who was suffering from kidney disease, stepped forward and asked that we pray for her to be moved up on the waiting list for a kidney transplant. The class responded enthusiastically to praying for her, but both they and Donna were puzzled when I suggested that perhaps we could take a slightly different approach. "Why don't we work to heal the kidneys you already have, Donna?" I asked.

She responded that I didn't understand her particular type of kidney disease, advising us that it was so rare that seldom, if ever, was it healed. She asked that we stick to praying for her original request of being moved up on the transplant list.

At this juncture, a story Alan Watts tells about how he was learning to "wait" and use "in between" moments for meditation popped into my mind. So I again suggested to Donna and the class that while we were "waiting" for her to be moved up on the transplant list, we experiment in the laboratory of prayer and see what we could do about her existing kidneys. Donna breathed a sigh of relief and said, "Okay."

I then asked the class, "How many of you woke up this morning and gave thanks for the perfect functioning of your kidneys?" As an assignment, I asked the students to give thanks every time they went to the bathroom and to simultaneously offer a prayer for Donna's kidneys. We called it the PP Prayer—praying while peeing. (Prayer is not reserved just for a certain room in the house, church, temple, mosque, or synagogue. Bathrooms are great for prayer.) I invited Donna to give thanks for her life and all of the ways in which her body temple serves her. I also gave her a daily reading assignment in *The Science of Mind* by Ernest Holmes, which specifically addresses the healing of kidneys.[3]

I had no knowledge about whether or not Donna applied the principle of gratitude or how the reading materials resonated with her, but a few months later she tearfully informed me that her kidneys spontaneously began normal functioning. Her healing befuddled the same doctors who had earlier prescribed a transplant as her only hope for survival. Today, two years later, Donna's kidneys are still normal, and she continues to be grateful for things most people take for granted. As Meister Eckhart, the Dominican monk and mystic observed, "A person can almost be defined by his or her attitude toward gratitude." Gratitude is powerful, leading Eckhart to also say, "If the only prayer you said in your whole life was 'thank you,' that would suffice."[4] Evolved people are grateful.

**EVOLVED PEOPLE GIVE WITHOUT AGENDA**

Evolved people give to live until they live to give. As individuals expand their understanding of universal law, they learn to give in order to live a life of inner wealth. They understand that they live in an opulent universe that seeks instruments through which to give of its unconditional love, compassion, lovingkindness, and resources. This is a process of growing out of a mindset of getting something from the world to *letting something from within you be freely given*. Generosity takes you off living on the "me" plan or the "we four and no more" plan, so consider putting yourself on a giving program that provides evidence that you are a generative being, that your generosity is a microcosmic reflection of the macrocosmic givingness of the Spirit. By the way, the word *generous*is from the Latin *generosus*, which is characterized by a noble spirit.

When I was a child and up until my teens, my grandmother and grandfather would visit my family. We always looked forward to their visits because we knew it meant that our beloved grandfather would slip us a silver dollar, which, by then, had become a collector's item. His gift was always accompanied with a mini-sermon: "Michael, if the world were divided into two kinds of people—givers and takers—always rush to be on the side of the givers, and you will discover that the Big Man upstairs will always take care of you." I speak from experience when I say he proved to be right, because the Spirit works through givers in ways beyond imagining.

Now when I suggest that you become more giving, I'm not talking about selling your house and giving away all your money. No. I'm describing a way to move from selfishness to selflessness. Before you begin your day, make it part of your spiritual strategy to ask yourself, "How can I give of myself today?" A few days of this practice and you will fall in love with giving, and universal law will respond by corresponding and give you even more to share with the world. Contemplate those ways in which you may share your time, energy, talents, skills, and financial resources with others. Then see how your heart becomes as wide as the world as you include your brothers and sisters on the planet in your good. In other words, you are now living to give.

### EVOLVED PEOPLE RACE TO SEE WHO CAN FORGIVE FIRST

A competition worth entering is the race to see how quickly you can forgive because evolved people race to forgive first. When we lack a forgiving consciousness, we become deaf to the whisper in our heart saying, "Forgive them, for they know not what they do."[5] A lack of forgiveness broadcasts a signal to the universe that there is something that someone has done to cause a sense of lack within you. For example, let's say you have not received an apology you believe is owed you. Your emotional body, then, embodies the energy of lack. Because everything is energy, the energetic thought-form of lack outpictures in your experience in some form, such as debt.

The resistance to forgiving is an attachment to the need to be right. When we are unable to forgive others, it is an indication that we also find it difficult to forgive ourselves. The power of forgiveness is liberating because it removes obstructions to the flow of good into our life. Forgiveness is one of the most potent contributors to the transformation of our own life, as well as that of others.

When Jesus the Christ encourages us to forgive seventy times seven, he was indicating that the practice of forgiveness is to become *a way of life.* Keeping our hearts and minds free of the debris of resentment and animosity is vital to our spiritual awakening. A passage in the Hindu *Mahabharta* exhorts that, "Forgiveness is holiness; by forgiveness the universe is held together. Forgiveness is the might of the mighty; forgiveness is quiet of mind. Forgiveness and gentleness are the qualities of the Self-possessed. They represent eternal virtue."[6]

**VISUALIZATION AND FORGIVENESS**

There are three purposes for practicing visualization. The first, and perhaps the most widely practiced, is when individuals visualize the tenor of the life they want to live, including the standard of living they want in order to be happy. The second is when we practice what our Native American brethren teach about walking a mile in another's moccasins, which gives birth to compassion. The third is as a forgiveness practice.

A visualization technique I have taught that individuals say has been helpful in their forgiveness practice works like this: Locate a quiet place in your home where you can sit uninterruptedly for a few minutes. Sit in a position of power with your spine straight and shoulders back. Without dropping your shoulders, relax the front of your body, consciously opening and softening around your heart area. Gently bring before your mind's eye the image of an individual you wish to forgive. Mentally broadcast a message of forgiveness to them, such as, "I forgive you and set you free. Your actions no longer have power over me. I acknowledge that you are doing the best that you can, and I honor you in your process of unfoldment. You are free and I am free. All is well between us. Peace is the order of the day."

You may also adapt the wording of this exercise for situations in which you feel a person needs to forgive you for some hurt you may have caused, such as, "I know that within you there is an energy of forgiveness that forgives me and sets me free. My words and actions have no power over you. You are free and I am free. All is well between our spirits. Peace is the order of the day."

As you experiment with these two techniques, don't be surprised or discouraged if at first you feel insincere or struggle with meaning what you say. As you repeat your words of forgiveness with a willingness to truly open your heart, you will neutralize the emotion of resentment and be freed from it. Love is your natural state of being, and through this exercise you will tap into this deep root within you.

I've been told by practitioners of both versions of this forgiveness visualization that they have experienced an opening of the heart and a willingness to communicate with the party or parties involved. Often they reported that once they arrived at a place of genuine, wholehearted forgiveness, the other person contacted them, or the next time they saw him or her, they were able to communicate and resolve the conflict. However, direct contact is not required for the completion of the forgiveness process.

## EVOLVED PEOPLE EXPERIENCE LIFE AS A CELEBRATION RATHER THAN A PROBLEM TO BE SOLVED

Evolved people understand that there's a celebration going on throughout this great Universe and that *a cosmic celebration can be localized within you when you realize that life is not a problem to be solved but a magnificent mystery to be lived*. When you function at this octave, you realize that in a state of God-consciousness, problems are dissolved.

Let me describe what I mean by this. When you walk into a dark room, you don't beat the darkness out with a stick. You turn on the light and realize that the darkness didn't really exist; it was only an absence of light. This is what happens when we dissolve a problem. A problem is like the darkness: when we switch on the light of awareness, we see that the problem didn't really exist; it was simply an absence of the light of understanding, of discerning clarity. When we expand into a deeper level of understanding, a paradigm shift occurs that makes room for a new response to enter our awareness. What was earlier a "problem" is dissolved because we have aligned ourselves with our inherent luminosity, our inner light, which knows only possibilities to be discovered and activated. *Problems are a human predicament, not a divine one.*

When we are immersed in the depths of a problem, our situation is like the baby chick encased in its shell. As the chick evolves, the shell becomes a polluted and claustrophobic environment where its space, mobility, and plentitude are challenged. God does not step up to the plate and "solve" this problem for the chick. The solution has already been placed in the seed of the chick's existence—the chick pecks its own way out when it has sufficiently evolved to maintain a life outside the shell. And so it is with us. All that we need to peck our way out of any challenging predicament is already within us, awaiting activation by our taking self-responsibility.

Our human problems are emblematic of areas where we are being called to grow, to peck into a new paradigm. So when we are in the midst of a challenge, if we stop long enough to meditate and remind ourselves of our innate gifts of intelligence, wisdom, and peace, we contact that place within us that also knows there are no problems, only human neuroses which can be healed by spiritual discernment.

Think back to before you got immersed in your all-caught-upness of how serious life was supposed to be, before someone said, "Stop playing around and get serious." Before you bought into that nonsense, you had a highly charged sense of enthusiasm, joy, spontaneity, and lightheartedness. Even in the face of challenges you may currently have, your inexhaustible life force hasn't gone anywhere. Your innate capacity to handle all that comes to you in life hasn't gone anywhere. You just temporarily halted your awareness of it by getting hooked into your problem. Consider this your permission to stop being serious and resume play-volving—a high state of creativity—and celebrating on the great playground of life!

### EVOLVED PEOPLE TALK TO THEMSELVES AND NOT TO THE WORLD

Evolved people accept themselves. They don't try to run away from themselves or imitate others or be anyone else. They trust their inner guidance system to direct them in the areas in which they have yet to grow while knowing that they are already a uniquely beautiful expression of the Infinite. They don't look to the outside world to convince them they are worthy of existence, that they are acceptable in the eyes of the world. We can spend an entire lifetime trying to convince everyone around us of our lovability, our worthiness, talents, and skills.

So rather than talking to the world, initiate a conversation within yourself. Call it a dialogue between your self and Self. I'm not talking about paying lip service to affirmative statements because anyone can parrot, "I am perfect, whole, and complete." Affirmation and embodiment of that which you affirm are not the same thing, so let me clarify that I am talking about cultivating a pattern of leaning into your inner Self with confidence so that you can skillfully handle whatever arises in your life. If you gain the praise of the entire external world but do not have the validation that comes from the realization of your own fundamental goodness, you have lost your own blessing. As the wisdom of Luke indicates, "For what profit is it to a man if he gains the whole world and is himself destroyed or lost?"[7] There is no outer critic conspiring against you, only the beggar consciousness within you. When you know that you are the beloved of the universe, then all of the energy that you have been using to convince the external world of who you are will now be yours to use for the beauty of simply being yourself just as you are.

When you stop wasting time trying to convince the world of your worthiness, you will notice how much more energy you have to invest in becoming acquainted with your natural goodness. The more you talk to yourself and listen to your inner voice, rather than outwardly depending on feedback from others, you will discover that the external world replicates the inner agreement you have with yourself about who and what you are. Remember, evolved people talk to themselves and not the world.

### EVOLVED PEOPLE CHOOSE HAPPINESS OVER DRAMA

Evolved people do not require drama to know that they exist. They realize that they don't need to be at the center of crisis after crisis, whether real or imagined, in order to feel alive or get the attention they desire. They stop repeating the mantra, "I have drama, therefore I am." Drama is not required to get their juices flowing, or to hold the attention of other people. Evolved people do not sabotage their happiness with self-created drama.

Notice when your mind starts chattering and writing operas about people and situations in your life that haven't even happened. Because of the ego's sense of self-importance, it wants to protect itself, so we create "potential" conversations in our minds and rehearse our end of the discussion. This is how we stir up drama, and, before long, we're inwardly causing ourselves both head and heart aches, all because of our attachment to drama. The more your inner observer identifies the trigger-thoughts that cause you to spin off, the more skillful you will be in introducing a sense of humor into the whole process and redirecting your mind to the "now" moment and a more cheerful mindset.

Evolved people know that genuine happiness cannot be bought or sold. It cannot be forced upon us, nor can we force it upon others. Happiness is our true nature. We begin to exude happiness when we reach within to its source through the practice of meditation. In meditation, we drink copiously from the well of joy and cultivate a "yes" point of view. Then, when challenges arise, we meet them with confidence in our ability to respond skillfully, maintaining an inner happiness that cannot be hijacked by drama.

**EVOLVED PEOPLE UNDERSTAND THE VALUE OF DOWNTIME**

Evolved people know that downtime is one of the most valuable gifts they can give themselves. They have experienced that downtime is when their spiritual root system is strengthened by stopping outer activity and simply *being*. Downtime provides for fresh insights and revelations to occur because the discursive mind has slowed its endless stream of chatter.

Perhaps there is no greater intrusion into our downtime than ourselves. We feel pressure to stay informed and on top of things in our rapidly changing world. Meditation, contemplation, and nonaction seem time-wasting, even selfish. They cause unnecessary guilt because the pressure to "do" is emphasized so much more than the value of "being." Computers, Internet, e-mail, cell phones, Walkmans, iPods, updating YouTube and My Space sites, downloading to our MP3 players, all invade our downtime. It all seems so vitally necessary, so much so that we make downtime less and less of a priority in our lives. In our high-tech low-touch society, downtime equals boredom, while entertainment equals coolness. The truth is that constant entertainment permits us to escape from ourselves and keeps us from having to come face-to-face with the painful, messier aspects of our life. It also keeps us from being receptive to insights that would be the impetus for our growth and creativity. *Authentic rest is power.*

If we are planting a tree, we bury its seed in the soil so that it can germinate where it is dark, quiet, solitary. The seed is nourished by the nutrients in the soil. This time under ground is vital to the growth of roots and prepares the tree to experience life above ground with its rain, winds, and frost. Our spiritual root system requires the nutrients of the Infinite in order to be fully present for our life's experiences and to meet them with receptivity, clarity, intuition, and confidence. When we set aside downtime to meditate, pray, contemplate, introspect, and study, we find that joy, peace, love, generosity of heart, compassion, and giving are perennially in season.

By cultivating these seven practices of evolved people, an entirely new self will be revealed to us, a self that has been present all along. We will feel ongoing gratitude for the simple blessings in life, give without agenda, and selflessly serve others. A compassionate heart of forgiveness will go out from us as a blessing. We will no longer live as a mere problem solver but as a joyous celebrant of what it means to have a precious human incarnation. We will consistently choose happiness over drama, creating inner peace and a calm environment. Downtime will become a given in our lives, causing us to be captured by love, vision, flashes of creativity, tastes of bliss in meditation, and recognition that we are here to celebrate Existence.

Reality enters our experience as evolved people. Dominion, freedom, full-out living—this is our divine destiny. Rise up and claim it!

### Affirmation

*Right here and right now, I acknowledge myself as an ever-evolving being and surrender to the transforming touch of the Spirit. Throughout this day, I have dominion over my consciousness and happiness. Patience, forgiveness, and lovingkindness are the order of my day.*

### Embodiment

In the nowness of this moment, I take dominion over my life and align with the evolutionary impulse governing the universe. And it is from this consciousness that I claim for and about myself gratitude, simple and humble gratitude for the countless blessings in my life, those of which I am aware and those of which I am not. The Self-givingness of the Spirit shows up in every aspect of my life. So I am grateful for my body temple that is even now vibrant with health, vitality, and vigor. Harmonious energy flows through every organ, muscle, and fiber of my being. I give thanks for the beauty that surrounds me. To every individual in my life, I say "thank you" for loving me, for sharing yourself with me, for inspiring me, and for uplifting me on days when I could not see my own inner beauty. I give thanks for all the good that flows into my life.

From my heart, I send a blessing to all beings on the planet, to all creatures and elements of nature. From North to South, from East to West, may all beings be free from suffering and the causes of suffering. May they know joy and peace, the peace that passes all understanding. May they flourish and be safe and secure in their environments with clear, pure water to drink and plenty to eat. I know that their good and my good are inextricably intertwined because we emanate from the same Source. So I give thanks for the rain of blessings upon their lives simply because they are my brothers and sisters whose hearts desire the same peace, compassion, understanding, forgiveness, and joy that I seek. I send out a blessing right now that their highest potential is realized in this lifetime and that forever more they live in harmony with their inner spirit.

I forgive myself for the ways in which I have fallen short of that which I know myself to be. I forgive myself for any inadvertent hurt I have caused another. Where anyone needs my forgiveness, I freely offer it now to those I feel have offended me in any way. I sense their spirits and know that in their essential being they meant no harm. Forgiveness is the order of the day, freeing me from contaminants of resentment, animosity, and anger. Any grudges I have been harboring are dissolved into the nothingness from which they came, any misunderstanding on the part of my egoic self releases them completely. By this statement of forgiveness, I restore my heart to its natural state of love and my actions are now those of kindness, service to my fellow beings.

Where I once moved in darkness, I have now turned on the light of awareness. This divine light illuminates what appeared to be problems with solutions that serve the highest good of all concerned. I celebrate the liberating truth that Love-Intelligence guides the course of my life. I know that I am mothered by the universe, and so I celebrate!

I am no longer somber and serious, knowing that in a consciousness of joy, new visions, inspirations, and resolutions are revealed to me in language my heart understands and responds to. I make space for this in my awareness now, knowing that nothing within me inhibits its inflow. Oh, how sweet it is to be wrapped in the unconditional love of this Presence, which so loved me that it personalized itself as me. How precious Life is. I celebrate in this awareness and broadcast my joy to all with whom I come in contact.

Happiness lights my path. It is my natural state of being, and I give thanks for it. Where I once responded to circumstances and individuals with drama, I now realize that this does not serve others or me. Respect, patience, and an open heart are the skillful means with which I meet all experiences.

How good it is to rest in Thee. Meditation, prayer, and contemplation soothe my spirit. When I feel the call of the Spirit to turn within, I respond wholeheartedly. I know that time for myself, for communion with the Self, is not something to be earned. Inner rest is a natural state of being, and I practice it daily.

My inherent wholeness now takes precedence in my life, renews my spirit, and releases the greatness within me. I willingly break free from consensus thinking, conventional thinking. I walk hand in hand with excellence, generosity of spirit, gratitude. These qualities are not bound by circumstance. They are the natural state of my being. I know myself to be an ever-evolving being, and I give thanks for it.

## Notes

1. Daniel 7:14.
2. Matthew 6:28–30.
3. Ernest Holmes, *The Science of Mind* (New York: Penguin Group, 1998).
4. Meister Eckhart, *Sermons and Treatises*, ed. Maurice O'Connel Walshe (Rockport, Mass.: Element, 1992).
5. Luke 23:34.
6. Vana Parva Mahabharta, Section XXVII, trans. by Sri Kisari Mohan Gangali (Calcutta, India: Oriental Press, 1893).
7. Luke 9:25.

# 3
# TRANSPORTATION TO TRANSFORMATION

*I'm ready to listen now*
*I've heard your voice before*
*Your way has been calling me*
*Now I'm walking through the open door*

As a vital expression of Existence, you have entered an agreement with the universal scheme of things to evolve your highest potential and deliver your best on the planet in a unique and magnificent way. How fortunate we are to be implanted with not only the inner impulsion (involution) to awaken to our true nature and the nature of reality but also the capacity to put that spiritual process into action (evolution). The spiritual warrior's conscious surrender to each step is the bridge to fulfillment.

It seems paradoxical that our spiritual practice culminates in the realization that we have been enlightened all along! Despite appearances to the contrary, we have always been whole and complete. Accepting and working with this paradox without demanding a linear explanation is what it means to be a spiritual grownup, to be spiritually mature.

So what is it, then, that actually "transforms" within us? *Transformation occurs when identification with the egoic self is dropped through a conscious realization of the Authentic Self*. It is the process of breaking through the illusion of an existence separate from the Whole. Transformation is a movement of awareness away from limited thought forms into a conscious realization of our limitless nature.

As we surrender more and more deeply to the transformative process through our spiritual practices, we realize that we cannot expect the outer conditions of our lives to change while we remain inwardly the same. The ego, however, tells us that if we could just somehow manage to change others or the irritating details of our environment, we ourselves won't have to change. This trickster ego employs many techniques. It may try to convince us that by beginning a new job or finding a new relationship, we will finally be at peace. If we move to a new city, we will have a geographical healing. New friends, lovers, and an employer will finally appreciate us. Even if we succeed in improving an external situation and gaining some temporary relief, nothing has actually transformed. Eventually, we are forced to face what we sought to avoid in ourselves. This is what is known as the wisdom of no escape.

## THE DIFFERENCE BETWEEN IMPROVEMENT, CHANGE, AND TRANSFORMATION

Improvement indicates that something has upleveled itself, like food packaging that advertises, "New, improved consistency." Perhaps something positive added to our lives, such as exercise, improves our blood pressure. If we were to abandon the habit of exercise, our blood pressure would return to its previous count. Or maybe we have a quick temper and have learned to count to ten before speaking. But if we forget to count, we may once again lose our temper. Improvement is always subject to fluctuation.

Change occurs when something shifts in our consciousness along with a corresponding change in our behavior. Stopping an addiction is change. When facing circumstances that previously triggered an addictive reaction, we no longer regress to our former behavior for handling whatever was emotionally triggered. We no longer bite the old hook because we have genuinely changed. While constructive change uplevels our inner and outer experience, if we regress in consciousness, old patterns may reassert themselves. Therefore, change is not permanent, nor is it transformation. Transformation includes change, but change does not include transformation. In other words, change has its limits since it stems from human will, while transformation is *limitless* since it stems from an evolving discovery and expression of the Authentic Self. (Note: *Full expression of the Authentic Self contains the dynamic of creativity and other qualities that seek expression through you.*)

## INTENTION AND ATTENTION: YOUR TICKET TO TRANSFORMATION

Take this noble journey. You will encounter detours, no doubt, but rely on the tools of intention and attention to get you back on track. The power of intention creates. The power of attention maintains our focus on our creative intention. Our intentions inform the direction of our attention. Use their powerful energy consciously and wisely because they are your ticket to transformation.

Notice where you consistently place your attention. Where we invest the energy of our attention determines the type of people, places, and conditions we manifest. Transformation requires that our attention align with our intention. When attention and intention conjoin, a powerful vortex of awareness is generated that keeps us mindful and in the "now" moment. Mindful attention allows us to make moment-by-moment choices that support our intention to transform.

Transformation occurs when we think and act from our true nature, which has no habits, no addictions, no likes or dislikes, which is simply pure being. So when we express a quality, such as love, it is unencumbered without expectation of receiving something in return. It is agenda-less; it is love for its own sake. When we transform, we retain all that is authentic in our human personality, even endearing little quirks, but we no longer cause harm to ourselves or to others.

**TOWARDS TRANSFORMATION**

Transformation that burns the seeds of old patterns of thoughts and actions requires disciplined commitment on our part. The first step is to root our motivation in a conscious intention to evolve, which gives us the spiritual backbone strong enough to take an honest look in the mirror of introspection. The universe constantly provides feedback through all of our interactions and circumstances, showing us those areas in which it would be to our evolutionary advantage to shift attitudes, perceptions, opinions, concepts, and beliefs. So we must be willing to stand before the tribunal of our own introspection with compassion and lovingkindness for what we observe. Then we must have the readiness for the rug of habitual thought patterns and actions to be pulled out from under us. Even though this is not especially comfortable, a spiritual warrior understands the liberating advantage of not being held hostage by the ego's tricks.

When first boarding the transportation to transformation, we ride a kind of spiritual high that we want to hang out in as long as possible. It's as though we have entered a grace zone. All of the energy that we formerly invested in playing it safe, in holding it all together is released, and we breathe more deeply. We inwardly relax, creating a gap for insights, breakthroughs—those "ah-ha" moments—to occur. *As compelling as this is, we are not here to get high; we are here to get free.* Transformation gets us free. Freedom happens by releasing the limiting beliefs and thought forms of the inner voice that says things like, "I'm too old to change," or "My color is holding me back," or "My parents will never forgive me for changing my spiritual path," or "I don't have enough education," or "It's just my bad karma," or "It must be God's will," or "I'm too busy to meditate today"—those well-rehearsed excuses we use to prevent ourselves from moving forward.

A genuine intention to transform is an invitation for spiritual lightning to strike and reveal our self-sabotaging habits, pointing us in the direction of what must be released so that we may evolve into our next dimension of being. When challenges arise and we face them with absolute trust in the fundamental goodness of the universe, tangible evidence is given to our trust in the process of transformation. Yes, there are bills to be paid. Yes, there are things that may be going on in the body temple, at work, or in a relationship. When we surrender to the evolutionary thrust of life by trusting, by having faith, we are given the wisdom to know that circumstances we call challenges and those we call blessings are both vital parts of the journey. In spite of appearances, we are not left alone to make our transformation or discover our true identity. Everything in the universe conspires toward supporting our self-realization. Throughout our entire existence, we are held in invisible arms of unconditional love, compassion, and immeasurable grace.

## TRACKING OUR PROGRESS

One of the things that we look for are "signs" along the way that we're "doing it right." If we're devoting a serious amount of time to our spiritual practices, it's natural for us to want some indicators that it's working. Fortunately, the benevolence of the universe provides such feedback all along the journey. *One strong indicator that we're making progress is that we are no longer inflated by praise or deflated by criticism.* We take neither personally, whether negative or positive in nature. We understand that one aspect of the ego's job description is to demand attention so that it can continue to believe in its existence. As we begin to break the ego's stranglehold over us, we notice that praise and blame no longer affect us as they did in the past.

A second indicator of progress is how quickly we are able to forgive ourselves and others. Resentment, animosity, and retaliation give way to compassion, self-forgiveness, and forgiveness of others. We more easily set aside our need to be right. We actually begin to be grateful to those who may have hurt us because they reveal those areas where we still cling and want to do things our way and our stubbornness toward change. We also create space for others to be who they are without the need to rearrange, manipulate, or control them according to our design. We drop the notion that others have been created to fulfill us, to make us happy, because we understand that no one is the cause of our happiness and that no one is the property of another person.

Our gratitude increases toward those who stand by us throughout our growth process—which can be quite messy—and we become more vulnerable, letting ourselves be seen as we are.

## MEDITATION: THE ART OF MIRRORING YOUR ORIGINAL FACE

If we want to travel to a certain destination, say the Cayman Islands, we can take a ship, a catamaran, or a jet plane. Likewise, there is transportation to transformation of varying speeds and efficiency. The choice is yours, and there is no judgment about how long you decide to take. If you want to stop along the way and enjoy the scenery, that is your choice. If you desire a faster arrival, then you will choose a more efficient mode of transportation and take a direct route.

The most efficient transportation to inner transformation is the practice of meditation. In meditation, we observe that thoughts come and go, emotions come and go. We catch that we are not our thoughts or emotions. We see that everything is that which breaks up into change—nothing remains the same—except that which observes change within us. The Authentic Self is the observer of change, the You who watches the constantly changing scenery of your mind and life. The inner witness is a dimension of who and what we really are. If you look within yourself, you won't find an accountant, actress, writer, husband, wife, mother, father, daughter, or son—not even a spiritual seeker! You will find the Self, which has no name, no label. This is consciousness, the soul of you, what the Buddha called the Witness. In meditation, we have the opportunity to watch our own mind, to become intimate with its mix of contents, and to experience its organic clarity, strength, and peaceful abiding. *Meditation leads to conscious use of the mind rather than being used by it.* As Osho wisely observed: "Remember, the head as a slave is a beautiful slave, of much utility. But as a master it is a dangerous master."[1] Meditation is a complement to any spiritual tradition and an exquisite practice for opening the heart to oneself and others.

Meditation blows back your hair, and you glimpse what Buddhists refer to as your original face—your natural goodness, your true identity—perhaps for the very first time. You begin to be more comfortable being spontaneous because you catch that your inner goodness is a reflection of the Spontaneous Goodness of the universe. As the world of phenomena spins round and round, revealing the constantly changing landscape of events, your inner happiness remains unchanged because it is not dependent upon or solely identified with the external aspects of life. You remain anchored in that which is changeless, the eternal Spirit of Life out of which you have come.

Self-realization, enlightenment, nirvana—these are attempts to express what defies description. Such teachers as Jesus the Christ, Bhagavan Krishna, Guatama Buddha, their disciples, the saints, sages, and mystics of the world's wisdom traditions who have reached the state of awakened consciousness have concocted words and definitions to inspire and motivate us to begin our own individual journey. Stepping onto the transportation to transformation is more seductive when the human mind can identify a purpose, so descriptions fuel our enthusiasm, our commitment, and nourish our hearts.

When choosing your transportation to transformation, your choices will determine the progress you make. Explore, experiment in the laboratory of your own consciousness and life. Whether you decide on a single vehicle or transfer to several modes of transportation surrender fully to each one so that you give to life all the gifts you have come to share and receive all that you so richly deserve.

### Affirmation

*I fully recognize and activate my power to set clear and potent intentions. My attention is inwardly directed, and I receive intuitive guidance in language my heart can understand and respond to. In gratitude, I surrender and trust where the Spirit is leading me in my intention to transform.*

### Embodiment

The spirit of the living God already knows my completion, my transformation. These are the only thoughts it has about me. My conviction of this truth and the actions I take are my transportation to transformation. The power of my intention to grow and expand in consciousness is heaven opening up its window to me. I enter that meditative space right here, right now, and enter my inner heaven of joy, inspiration, peace, and wisdom. As I sit and observe the contents of my mind, I breathe in acceptance of the work I am to do to transform by the renewing of my mind through the power of intention and attention.

As discursive thoughts arise that are not aligned with my intention, I calmly discard them without judgment. They have no power over me. Only the Spirit has full sway over my life and guides my steps. Spirit is in the midst of me and lovingly guides my path to awakened consciousness. (Pause and feel into that statement. Breathe into it and remain still for five minutes or longer.)

I feel and sense my oneness with this Presence. I sing from a place of awareness, I dance from it, and I am silent in it. I pray from this state of consciousness, knowing that as I intentionally speak this word, a movement in consciousness stirs within me a realization that innate wholeness, abundance, prosperity, health, and peace are the spiritual birthright of all beings.

Intention and surrender even now free me. There is nothing inhibiting this divine flow. It's happening now. I feel it in my bones and give thanks for it. These moments of quietude reveal to me the grand design of the universe and my place in it. I respond to this knowledge and get out of the way of it happening in, through, and as me. I move from potential to actuality. Fulfillment is occurring. It blows back my hair and reveals my original face. I am now becoming more of myself. As I continue to turn within, I realize that I am becoming the individual that I've always wanted to be. There's more love, more harmony, more patience and humility, more generosity, beauty, and creativity.

My field of perception is widening and my spiritual vision is increasing. I free myself from the clutches of the ego and make space for the universe to become conscious of itself as me. (Pause for several moments and enter the feeling tone of that truth statement. If your attention begins to wander, gently bring it back to the breath.)

Transformation is the field on which I play, work, love, create, give, and serve. As the world of phenomena spins 'round, I release all that would inhibit the fulfillment of the revelations I receive in this period of meditation. As I take my next holy breath, I establish an intention from the depth of my being. I wrap my entire consciousness around it and infuse it with my enthusiasm, my willingness to surrender anything that would block its activation in my life. (Pause and state your intention aloud or silently. Repeat your intention several times, infusing it with the energy of conviction and confidence.)

I take another breath and allow this intention to take firm root in my consciousness. Every thought, feeling, and perception is saturated with my commitment to this intention. I bathe my mental body, emotional body, etheric body, and physical body in my intention and give it my full attention.

As a spiritual warrior, my courage to face all that is required for my transformation is embodied with grace and ease. This is a prayer that is heard and responded to by universal law. Beyond human reasoning, beyond intellect, even beyond appearances, I throw open my heart and make room for a great transformation to unfold within me and express through me.

From this moment on everything unfolds in a most magnificent way. I release myself into this great excellence and simply let it be. And so it is.

## Note

1. Osho, *Intelligence: The Creative Response to Now* (New York: St. Martin's Press, Griffin, 2004).

# 4
# From Reel to Real

*I'm ready to run*
*And I'm ready to leap into what is real*
*I got a sweet invitation, a mandate of ecstasy*

The universe is forever sending out a casting call to us to accept our starring role in an A-list movie: stepping out of the movie reel version of our life and accepting the real role of who and what we are—our Authentic Self. As we sit in our inner screening room observing the moment-to-moment changing scenery of our life, we may wonder what indeed is the part we have come to play on this great stage of life. Only spiritual technology is advanced enough to edit our current points of view, to cut our illusions about what is real, and to leave them on the cutting room floor of consciousness. *Most people do not experience Reality but rather their thoughts about Reality*. However, our thinking about Reality does not put us in touch with the Real. Reality enters our awareness when we awaken to our Authentic Self. When authenticity itself speaks through our words, thinks through our thoughts, walks through our feet, serves through our hands, and loves through our hearts, our lives have become Real.

The mind provides the film on which we record the movie of our life. When watching this movie, if we are honest, we can see that its theme is what we think reality is, which probably deserves about a two-star rating. "I've been playing this part for thirty-five years," we self-proclaim. "It's a wrap—and all within my karmic budget." We're practically ready to ask for our own autograph! I've heard professional actors say that they can become so self-identified with a role that they actually forget their character is not real. I read about an actor who played Moses. He had so merged his personality with his part that even after the movie was in the theaters, he still walked around with a staff and wore a beard. You may have heard or read interviews with actors who've said they've been typecast in a specific role so often that their agents and fans can't see them playing another one. In the theater of life, we too can become so identified with the parts we play that we can't imagine being anyone other than the surface persona we have created and present to the world.

Of course, we also audition others and assign them roles to play in our life's epic. These additional actors are needed so that we can project onto them characteristics and actions for which we don't want to take responsibility. "They" are the bad guys, the monsters, the villains who make us our movie's hero or heroine. When scenes of negativity are projected onto the screen of our life, we exclaim, "Oh, that's my mother's fault," or "My ex-husband made me do it," or "My boss just doesn't understand me." But this is the result of a fuzzy camera lens. When we refocus with objectivity, we see the facts more clearly and become willing to take self-responsibility for our life's circumstances. We spiritually mature and drop the blame game. We realize that there is no one to blame, only ignorance.

## ACCEPTING THE ROLE OF THE AUTHENTIC SELF

When we begin to feel claustrophobic in our movie, it is an indication that we have outgrown our part, which causes us to review our role, to look at it afresh. With clarity of view, we can begin shedding the ego's false sense of self-importance and accept the part of a lifetime: the Authentic Self. The transition from the egoic self to the Authentic Self requires discipline, which all skilled actors have. The good news is that discipline eventually becomes what I call a "blissipline" because it leads to playing our part with integrity, dignity, elegance, passion, and deep contentment.

Sometimes, however, even when we know that it's time to quit a role, we postpone due to suffering from "analysis-paralysis." The symptoms include rounds of relentless questioning, such as, "What if I don't like my next part? What if it stretches me further than I'm comfortable going? What if no one likes me in my new role?" This is when it's time to sit down, get in touch with our inner set designer, and haul out the prop of self-discipline.

## THE "BLISSIPLINE" IN DISCIPLINE

We've all experienced how discipline sometimes causes an automatic rebellion or resistance within us. We don't like the energy around the word *discipline*, perhaps because of the place it has occupied in our upbringing, education, or religion. However, a healthy view of discipline keeps us on track in areas of our life where we've determined to make a change. *Discipline is a practice of self-love, self-respect, and surrender that results in freedom.*

Let's say, for example, that you've decided to incorporate a daily practice of meditating before you leave for work each morning. You love the results you get from the times you do meditate—clarity, stability, strength, communion with the Self—and you're now willing to do what it takes to make it a daily part of your morning routine. Everything is going along just fine when, out of the blue, your mate can't take the children to school in the morning and you have to pitch in for a couple of weeks. Instead of getting up just a little earlier in the morning to accommodate this new responsibility and still have time to meditate, you tell yourself, "Oh, I just don't feel like it, and, besides, I need my rest." What happened? Your emotional reasoning justified your decision not to make the necessary effort to honor your aspiration to meditate every morning.

The gift of self-discipline is that it has the power to take you beyond the reasoning of temporary emotion to freedom. Think of how empowered you've felt on occasions when you haven't given in to the "I don't feel like it" syndrome and honored your commitment to yourself. What does not *feeling* like it have to do with it? The combination of love for something with the willingness to do what it takes to practice it—discipline—results in freedom.

An evolved practice of discipline is essential for success in any arena of life. When applied to the spiritual path, discipline is a skillful, precise art. The root of the word *discipline* means to discern, to perceive clearly. I like what Osho wrote about discipline in his book *Love, Freedom, and Aloneness*: "To be a disciple means to learn the discipline of being yourself, your true self."[1]

During one of my meetings with His Holiness the Dalai Lama, a rare opportunity opened up to have the blessing of a few moments of just hanging out with him. To me, he is a wonderful example of the freedom that comes from the practice of discipline. Although exiled from his own country and saddened by the tragedy occurring in Tibet, he radiated tremendous love, peace, and joy. In fact, I got a great photo of my wife, Rickie, and him together. They were trying to get into a more formal pose when I called out to Rickie, "Look at the Dalai Lama and sing, 'Hello Dalai! Good to see you, Dalai'." They began laughing uncontrollably, and I got a wonderful photo of them. Both he and Rickie were laughing the spontaneous laugh of Buddha. Rickie was a little disappointed because she wanted a "spiritual" photo. My take on it was that catching this being of pure joy laughing couldn't be more perfect.

What I admired on that occasion was how the Dalai Lama openly expressed his feelings about the suffering of the Tibetan people, whom he profoundly loves, and how, in the next instant, a smile of transcendence would light up his face. Even as he spoke out against what is happening in his country, he was not entrapped by that experience. He did not freeze-frame the scene. In his wisdom, he realized that life is fluid, that those who suffer today can be free tomorrow. He pierced the veil of appearances and saw Reality. I attribute this in great measure to his daily discipline of meditation, which gives him the spaciousness of inner freedom. He was able to stand in Reality while responding compassionately to the distressing circumstances of his people. He did not deny the reality of what was happening in Tibet or the Reality of his inner freedom.

The inner work we are called to do is no different from His Holiness the Dalai Lama's. We too are candidates for enlightenment, for entering pure Reality. Through the inner discipline of meditation, we are able to break through the density of the three-dimensional realm in which we live to become genuinely free.

Each of us has the choice to write the discipline of freedom into our daily script. It is wise to do so because such a practice strengthens our spiritual backbone. Just as we surrender to the disciplines required by our profession to achieve our career goals, so are we to surrender to the discipline required on our spiritual quest. Sometimes, however, when it comes to spiritual discipline, our ego gets ruffled because the free reign it has had over us is now challenged, even threatened. Ego mistakes freedom as doing whatever it wants whenever it wants. The pompous ego does not want to be revealed for what it is: the author of fear-based roles founded on the false premise of a self that is separate from the Whole.

When we sincerely apply ourselves to our spiritual practice, we give up the ego-props which we have used as the backdrop for our life's experiences. We open ourselves to introducing new inner and outer scenery. What we think, say, and do become opportunities to reflect the Real. *After all is said and done, without the Real, the reel would not exist in the first place!* What we want to achieve through practicing the discipline of freedom is to free ourselves from our all-caught-upness and live in awareness of the Divine Light without which there could be no movie called life.

Regardless of where you stand in your evolutionary process, the capacity to enter Reality is always available to you. Call it a renewal, redemption, resurrection, transfiguration, or transformation—it doesn't matter. The freedom of discipline means that you agree to free yourself from the limitation of playacting the roles assigned to you by society, family, religion, and education and accept the part that has been written for you since the beginning of time: being your Self.

### YOUR FEATURE ROLE IN *EARTH WALK*

Some of us are of an age that we can remember going to movie theaters at a time when you could look back to the projection room window and follow the beam of light from the movie projector right onto the screen. All of the characters on the screen seemed so real that you could be brought to tears, laughter, fear, and delight. Yet, if you turned around and followed the beam of light back to the projection room, you could see that it was nothing but a play of light. The characters were never really alive on the screen, only the light was there.

The movie featured in our three-dimensional Earth theater is projected from the Light of the Ineffable onto the screen of Life. Each of us has a feature role in this movie titled *Earth Walk.* Consciousness is the Light that projects the film onto the screen of our awareness. When we sit in deep meditation and interior prayer, we attune ourselves to that Light and an opening is created for us to move from the movie reel version of our life into the Real joy of existence.

*Most of the time, we are experiencing a movie about what we believe life to be, not what it actually is.* When things get a little too dull for the ego, we consciously or unconsciously stir up drama. But as we begin to move from the movie reel version of our life to the Real, we realize that we write, edit, and finalize our own script. Our assignment is to play our part well with gusto, creativeness, passion, and juice, all the while understanding that we are the Light from which we have come and to which we return after the curtain goes down on this incarnation. May each and every one of us enthusiastically, with whole-souled commitment, take our cues directly from our Source and joyously dance together on this stage called Life.

### Affirmation

*Right here and right now, I rebirth the Real in my awareness.*
*I activate clear seeing and allow it to light my way in all that I think, say, and do throughout this day.*

*I play my part on the stage of life with gusto, openhearted joy, and wisdom.*

### Embodiment

In this moment, I move into a celebratory consciousness, a grateful consciousness for the realization that as I surrender my life to the Real, it is made more and more manifest in my experience, placing me in alignment with what Is. With the simplicity of a child, I embrace the Real, even as it embraces me.

I hear with my inner ear the part I am to play in each area of my life. As I surrender to this guidance, I am not robbed of my individuality; I am freed from the sway of my ego that would glorify itself. So I turn with complete confidence to the Presence within and hear it say, "When you place your attention on that which is Real, you will behold your original face, your true nature of Wholeness."

In my sense of individuality I know that I am undivided from the Whole. And knowing I am undivided from the whole, I proclaim that all of my needs are met on every level of my existence. There is divine peace. There is divine order. There is abundance, health, vitality, safety, and security. There is harmony and creativity. I am bold enough to accept this. I am confident enough to witness to the presence of the living God within and around me. This is the Reality upon which I rely, knowing that it transcends any paradigms of lack, limitation, and not enoughness. The divine life that I am transcends all diagnosis and prognosis. I begin again, right now, and step into Reality.

I honor the integrity of my spirit and court the best that is yet to come, the next stage in my evolution. I accept that it is safe to embrace and express my Authentic Self. Into the field of the sacred "yes," my every cell, every organ, every action and function of my body, mind, and spirit is made whole. All of my relationships are shot through with unconditional love, compassion, joy, and purpose.

Discipline becomes a blissapline because I realize it leads to my ultimate freedom. During good times and challenging times, I meditate without attachment to the fruits of my practice. Whether peace or restlessness is the undercurrent of my practice, it is my offering of love to the Spirit. I sit and practice for the love of it, not simply to gain merit or experience a spiritual high. I meditate to walk through the door of freedom and know that I am welcomed by an all-loving Presence.

I go forth and joyously play my part without attachment to the fruits of my actions. I offer them to the Spirit as an act of love. I bow before the Reality of the life that is within me, beating my heart, breathing my breath, moving me from one place to another. For this and so much more, I am so utterly grateful and simply allow it to be.

## Note

1. Osho, *Love, Freedom, and Aloneness: A New Vision of Relating* (New York: St. Martin's Press, 2001).

# 5
# Transcending the Tyranny of Trends

*When you're born of the Spirit*
*You're made so brand new*
*And all the time you wasted*
*Is given back to you*

There is a cosmic magnet drawing each of us into an intimate exploration of the dimensions of our being. And yet, few of us have responded to this magnetic pull and intimately communed with our deepest Self. The word *intimacy* comes from the Latin root *intimum* and refers to our innermost core. When we give our consent to this mystical adventure, we open ourselves to the wonders of existence, which are so exquisite we are metaphorically brought to our knees.

What I'm describing here is not some spiritually romantic notion. A profound inner search is an adventure for the spiritually courageous, for the spiritual warrior. It is an inner trek that takes us down roads of self-discovery we have not walked before. It is where nothing is avoided—the ecstatic and the profane—everything is faced. This is how we embrace the fullness of who we are and come into genuine self-acceptance. We break through the filters through which we view and live life. Those filters include our past fears, our hopes for the future, all the ego's cherished opinions, beliefs, and concepts that we use to hold our life together. Our "yes" to participating in this journey is our entrance into a consciousness of beholding.

## THE NON-DUAL PRACTICE OF BEHOLDING

*Beholding* is a state of consciousness in which we experience clear seeing. The ego recedes and our inner view of the outer world is as though we were tasting Reality for the first time. We come face-to-face with *what is* with no need to alter or filter it.

Imagine what you might experience if you applied the Buddhist koan, "Show me the face I had before my parents were born." As you invite the universe to mirror your original face, you are in substance saying, "Show me the glory that has been mine since the beginning of existence." Leaving behind any preconceived notions of what that would look like, as your inner vision comes into focus, you will shake off the illusory dust and grit of the outer journey and begin a most excellent beholding from within. You behold that you are in league with excellence, that there is a sacred pact, a covenant with the qualities encoded in your spirit, such as love, beauty, order, harmony, peace, wisdom, compassion, creativity, nobility, joy—all the non-dual qualities which are your spiritual birthright.

We have been given this precious human incarnation in which each and every one of us is a candidate for enlightenment. The beauty of the human experience is that we may consciously behold the Self of us. But in order to arrive at this awakened state, you must want it like a drowning man craves breath. Consider this: doesn't an inquiry into the purpose of existence deserve your time and attention? Within the twenty-four hours of each day, one-twenty-fourth can surely be devoted to becoming acquainted with the inner Self.

Some consider this "navel-gazing,"—a word meaning self-absorption that became popular during the 1960s when meditation began to take hold in the West. Individuals who subscribe to this definition have not realized that this is not self-interest; it is interest in existence.

## LEVELS OF BEHOLDING

There are various levels of beholding. First, we learn to focus our attention. We get to choose that upon which we focus our attention and how we invest our energy. Next, we enter meditation and deeper states of interior awareness and begin to open the door to beholding the sacredness of life. We learn that life is all for us, and nothing is against us.

Have you ever noticed the glow of things around you after a period of meditation? Many shamans, yogis, and saints see with the inner eye the astral energy, the life force that is not visible to the human eye, sustaining nature and human life. They have walked through walls, appeared in two places at the same time, been buried alive under ground for weeks. The bodies of some Catholic mystics remained incorruptible in the face of seeming death. Such beings mastered the art of beholding. In the beholding state of consciousness, they consciously directed the life force, which is how Jesus performed miracles. He beheld in consciousness the truth that life is Spirit's energy condensed into the world of matter, governed by cosmic laws. Because his consciousness was one with this truth, he had mastery over the physical realm. He worked the law of buoyancy when he caused his body to energetically vibrate lighter than water so that he could walk upon it. He reinvigorated Lazarus's life force, causing his body temple to re-activate itself. Having a spiritually scientific law that explains such miracles is not dismissive of Jesus as a fully illumined master. Although he attained self-mastery, he is no different from you or me. Our mandate is to start right where we are and begin our practice of beholding our true nature.

A deeper level of beholding can occur when you ask questions, such as, "Where is the self that is feeling hurt, irritated, fearful?" Meditation and contemplation show you how such a self cannot be found because it does not exist other than as a temporal, ephemeral identity. Fear, anxiety, doubt—these are thought forms and emotions that pass through the mind like a cloud in the sky. Unless we hook into them, download them so that they become concretized in our mind, they will simply float through and dissipate.

Eventually you will wake up to the realization that your Authentic Self has never been nor can be hurt, harmed, or endangered, despite appearances to the contrary. That is a paradox of life. As Bhagavan Krishna said to his disciple Arjuna in the *Bhagavad Gita* concerning the nature of the soul, "No weapon can pierce the soul; no fire can burn it; nor water can moisten it; nor can any wind wither it."[1] And in a later verse we read, "This Self is never born nor does it ever perish; nor having come into existence will it again cease to be. It is birthless, eternal, changeless, ever the same, unaffected by the usual processes associated with time."[2] This describes our original face, our Authentic Self.

We have taken a human incarnation to behold the gifts of divinity that are within us, to dissolve any sense of separation from the power, presence, and love of the Spirit. The choice is yours to remain under the tyranny of trends or do the inner work necessary to enter the consciousness of beholding your Authentic Self. Self-realization is never forced upon us.

**FREEDOM FROM THE TYRANNY OF TRENDS**

One of the ways we hijack our capacity to experience a state of beholding is that we become swept up in what I call the "tyranny of trends." The tyranny of trends allows for the lowest common denominator to set the standard of success and, of course, "coolness." Very often, trends convince individuals what their life's priorities should be. The tyranny of trends is blasted out at us from television, radio, newspapers, tabloids, computers, and even our dentist's waiting room, attempting to convince us that we must smell a certain way, wear a certain label, weigh a specific weight, have whiter teeth, drive a certain car, make a certain income, and so on, before we can consider that we've "made" it.

You've no doubt heard or read about how Americans are considered the most entertained individuals on the planet, people who know more about what a superstar had for breakfast than the ingredients of their own first meal of the day. The reach of the tyranny of trends is far-flung. I travel a lot and so I spend a great deal of time in airports, which have become shopping malls. Whether I'm in parts of America, Europe, or the villages of Brazil, Africa, or India, cell phones and other "infotainment" are in full operation. But shopping seems to be the "waiting for the plane" entertainment of choice.

I like to people-watch in airports, and when I read the energy on shoppers' faces, what I sense is that they are in search of something to want. *They shop not so much because they actually need something, but in an unconscious state of wanting to want something*. So often people just want to want something, so they cruise the shops hoping that this "want" will reveal itself, that it will jump off the shelf and announce, "I'm what you want to want!" They miss the whole point that it is an inner fulfillment that their spirit longs to realize and express.

Many people are snared by this impulse. This inner urge that speaks to us of "want" originates in the still, small voice that is ever calling us to cultivate the want to be more ourselves. But the ego does a voiceover on it, which translates into a desire to grasp, to get ego satisfaction from shopping and other addictive behaviors. The innate desire to be your Authentic Self is hijacked by the ego. But as you become more mindfully aware, you will develop a sense of humor in dealing with the ego's tricks. You don't have to waste time feeling guilty when you catch yourself; laugh it off. Then you will bust the ego wide open, neutralize its false power, reveal it for what it is, stop wanting to want, and re-attune yourself to the wisdom of the still, small voice within.

All inner urges that do not find their fulfillment in the Self, in its oneness with the Universal Self, will be left unfulfilled. These urges are meant to be fulfilled creatively, through expressions of generosity, love, oneness, wholeness—you get the idea. Otherwise, they will seek fulfillment in consumerism, an ongoing unmet craving of wanting to want.

Ernest Holmes addressed this so wisely: "The very urge for personal gratification is incomplete until it finds a universal outlet."[3] What one has to do is turn within and ask, "What is the reason for my existence?" Ask sincerely, ask deeply, ask wanting to genuinely receive a response as to what is in your highest spiritual interest and the highest and best spiritual interest of all concerned. When you do so, you will discover that the meaning of "universal outlets" is those qualities and subsequent actions that lead to being a beneficial presence on the planet.

## REJUVENATE, REGENERATE, RESURRECT YOURSELF

We live in stressful times and are bombarded daily with bad news. In contrast, how little we hear about the trend of tremendous good that is being done, the trend of compassionate, generous humanitarian action that is occurring on the planet. Here's some good news: we have the power to unhook ourselves in this very instant, to drop the cell phone, the earplugs, the ear receiver, and just for a while, sit still and simply be. Not be someone, but just rest in our pure being. Of course we may become unrecognizable to ourselves, which can make us feel a little disoriented for a while. Nevertheless, I encourage you to take the risk because it's worth it; you're worth it.

Right on the ground where you now stand, dare to unhook from all of the complaining, excuses, projections onto others, blaming—all the rackets that we run in order to cope with life. It is absolutely within our ability to rejuvenate, regenerate, and resurrect ourselves. When we see or hear about others who have transcended their individual challenges, we can be confident that they have first transcended the tyranny of trends by beholding a deeper dimension of their innermost core.

## BIG GOD, OR BIG PROBLEM?

One obstacle to a consciousness of beholding is that we have been indoctrinated in the belief that God is the big problem-solver, a runner of earthly errands on our behalf, a caterer to all our material desires. We have an opinion of exactly what God should be doing for us, even setting a due date for when the goods should be delivered. This way of thinking limits the possibilities.

It is God to whom we pray to end wars, to be on "our side" of the war, to stop the scourge of genocide, the ravages of AIDS. This is an immature concept of the Godhead. We don't need to tell God about our big problem; we tell our problem about our big God!

In God-awareness, problems dissolve because there are no "real" problems; in the mind of God, there are only perfect patterns of existence and divine ideas. When we realize this, we begin to consciously apply spiritual laws and principles to our seeming problems and challenges.

### TRUST IS THE INSTRUMENT OF BEHOLDING

Many people have in their prayer life what might be called "spiritual temper tantrums." They believe that God is sitting on a throne in heaven with the purpose of raining down blessings upon them in the form of fulfilling their desires. If those desires remain unfulfilled, they lose faith. If we are honest, we will admit that sometimes our prayers and affirmations are more like foot-stomping demands that lack a surrendered spirit or take self-responsibility.

It is far more spiritually healthy to take an affirmative stance when dealing with life's challenges. While we may honestly acknowledge that we would prefer a certain outcome, it is essential to surrender our attachment to how we think our prayer should outpicture. Nothing is being withheld from us, and in spite of appearances, we are infinitely loved and treasured. Osho beautifully put it this way: "You are cherished by the whole. That's why the whole goes on breathing in you, pulsating in you. Once you start feeling this tremendous respect and love and trust of the whole in you, you will start growing roots into your being."[4] To trust is to behold the goodness of our Source, the goodness within cosmic creation, and that same inherent goodness within our very own Self. When we read the biblical story of creation in Genesis, after each day, the Creator's pronouncement was that it was "good and very good."[5]

### ENTER THE MATRIX OF CONSCIOUSNESS

Most of the time we do not experience Reality but, instead, our individual thoughts about reality. Reality cannot be analyzed or intellectualized; it can only be encountered in awakened awareness. Through meditation, contemplation, affirmative prayer, visioning, and spiritual study, we enter a matrix of consciousness that is our entry into clear seeing, our introduction to Reality. An entirely new world begins to reveal itself before our inner gaze. That real world has been there all along, but we have not accessed it because our priority has been the pursuit of externals, all the things we think we need to be happy, a byproduct of the tyranny of trends.

Our social conditioning has been to fit in, to fulfill society's expectations. We develop coping mechanisms, defense mechanisms, compulsive behaviors, and addictions that drown out the cry of the inner spirit seeking to be freed within us. We rehearse how we will respond, "... if he *ever* says that again, I'll make it absolutely clear he can't get away with that with me again!" A conscious or unconscious battle goes on inside to protect, defend, and exalt the egoic self. All we get from this effort is an advanced case of inflammation of the ego.

When we enter a consciousness of beholding, we no longer jump on life's ride of ups and downs. We become more impervious to the tyranny of trends. We become sensitized to the trend tyrant approaching or hanging around us, and we patiently work within ourselves to arrive at safer ground. Through spiritual practice, we acquire the ability to stabilize our mind during times when it wants to or does get all worked up. In the beholding state of consciousness, we attune ourselves to the elegance, order, intelligence, harmony, beauty, and luminosity of the Spirit. We then draw into our magnetic field people, places, and experiences that vibrate at this expanded level of consciousness. We begin to move from having thoughts about reality to a realization of the Real. Those who realize the Real know their innate wholeness is a reflection of cosmic wholeness.

## BREAKING THE EGOIC BONDS OF SEPARATION

So why do we imagine ourselves to be separate from the whole in the first place? The good news is that it's not our fault! It's not due to "original sin," or a plague cast upon humanity. In the Judeo-Christian ethic, we find an answer in Genesis, which says that immediately following the act of creation "there arose a mist."[6] This mist is what the Hindu and Buddhist scriptures refer to as *maya*, or illusion. It is the sense of separation from the whole, the mist of duality that we are subject to. We did not create it. It is part of the cosmic scheme of things that we break through this illusory fog and awaken to our true nature. This is the spiritual warrior's journey to a consciousness of beholding Reality.

## THE LAW OF BUOYANCY

Each of us is an individual expression of an unfolding collective, cosmic destiny. As we begin to understand this, we do our spiritual work with a deeper level of commitment, focus, and enthusiasm. We begin to consciously explore and participate in the laws governing the universe. The essence of life is invisible, and its laws are invisible. However, empirical evidence of their existence is revealed under the proper conditions when a proper container is provided.

Take for example the law of buoyancy, which of itself is invisible. If you place a properly constructed boat in any body of water it will float, revealing the existence of an invisible, universal law called buoyancy. You can't say, "My boat floats in American oceans, but in Tahiti, forget about it!" Universal laws are no respecter of persons, places, or things. The law of buoyancy works in all bodies of water for all people who have a properly constructed boat. Whether they are smugglers or the Coast Guard, their boats will stay afloat.

Unfortunately, our awareness is afflicted and obscured by beliefs in lack, limitation, self-importance, guilt, and shame, which prevent us from perceiving Reality. These are the result of the "mist" of duality and cause us to essentially say, "Well, I come from a family of non-floaters. My grandparents couldn't float and neither could my cousins. In fact, our whole hereditary line is filled with non-floaters. So please, get off my case about floating!"

We don't inherit such things as selfishness or hardness of heart from our families any more than we inherit generosity and compassion. We are, however, influenced by the thought patterns, beliefs, and habits inherent in the family environment and all social institutions that are invested in "socializing" the individual. *We don't inherit these things through bloodlines but rather through habitual thought-lines.* This is what the biblical statement means when saying that the iniquities of the parents are visited upon the children.[7] However, we have a cosmic heredity that supersedes all else. If we test the law of buoyancy under the proper conditions, we will float! Whether or not we have ever floated or if anyone else in our family has floated before is immaterial. During times when we become caught in the mist of doubt, lack, limitation, or scarcity, if we place ourselves in a state of beholding, we can free ourselves. Consciousness is buoyant.

## ASKING AERODYNAMICALLY SOUND SPIRITUAL QUESTIONS

Just as when an engineer builds an airplane and places its wings in a wind tunnel to assure that they are aerodynamically sound, so may we place aerodynamically sound questions in the wind tunnel of Universal Mind to assure that we will be lifted above the temporary experiences we pass through. For example, when a person falls into victim consciousness, they tend to ask, "Why me, God?" This is actually more of an accusation, a statement about our lack of self-responsibility wherein we blame conditions outside of ourselves. If we're an especially stubborn case, we don't investigate more deeply, so our experiences repeat themselves. This cycle will continue until we learn to ask more spiritually aerodynamic questions that will lift us out of the mist—the illusion—we've been living in. Examples of spiritually aerodynamic questions are: "What quality am I to cultivate to shift this circumstance in which I find myself? What skills am I being called to develop? What would Life have me do here?"

Negativity doesn't have a cause; it's merely a mist. If negativity had a cause, it would last forever; it could never be shifted. So-called negativity arises from the ego's sense of separation from the Whole. And not all pain is negative, even though we label all forms of pain as such and resist them. Positive-negativity is a circumstance that causes us to go deeper, to search ourselves, to stop placing blame on the causes of suffering outside of ourselves, and take self-responsibility.

Circumstances arise and hard times come so that we may grow through them, so that we may evolve. I like to say that *a bad day for the ego is a good day for the soul.* When we look back on some of our most challenging experiences, we admit that we wouldn't trade what we gained from them for remaining the same as we were. Something within acknowledges that during those times when we are pressed against the ropes of life, we learn to become more generous, to forgive, to never give up on ourselves or others. We learn to regenerate, to rejuvenate, to surrender.

## SURRENDER: THE STANCE OF THE SPIRITUAL WARRIOR

*Surrender is a bold spiritual stance, the stance of a spiritual warrior, because what we are surrendering to is the next stage of our evolution.* And as we surrender our all, we create the inner spaciousness for Life to be seen as it is. As egoic obscurations—such as doubt, fear, worry, self-importance, greed, and envy—are cleared, we become more and more of our Authentic Self. It's like LASIK—laser-assisted in situ keratomileusis—surgery, when the obscuring film is removed from the eyes, we see clearly. Likewise, when the obscuration of separation is removed from the inner eye, the mist is lifted and we see life clearly. We realize that there is only wholeness, oneness.

During those times when you realize that you are held hostage by the tyranny of trends, just laugh and be grateful that you busted yourself. This is the beginning of clear seeing. Give thanks that you have become sensitive enough to catch yourself right at the outset, before you got carried away. This is aerodynamic spiritual progress! You are beginning to enter the beholding state of consciousness, witnessing rather than reacting.

An advanced level of beholding is experienced as you grow into the realization that just as you are a hologram of infinite possibilities, so are others in your environment, whether or not they are conscious of it. You realize that just like you, they too long to know themselves, to be happy, to express their innate talents and skills. It may not appear that way, but we all have an innate desire to experience our spiritual birthright of *happiness*. Even the Constitution of the United States spells happiness with a capital H and guarantees our right to pursue it. What we really want is to realize it.

Begin to consciously break your agreement with the mediocrity present in the tyranny of trends. No longer consider trendsetters as people who are to be admired or imitated. Break free from the hold of what society tells us we should be like. Be drawn into the presence of those who exemplify the next level of human evolution—a spiritual teacher or spiritual community. Each of us has arrived on planet Earth to behold, to participate in the adventure of exploring the truth that we are enlightened beings having a human incarnation.

**YOU ARE AN ADVENTURER IN CONSCIOUSNESS**

Just as we meet different aspects of ourselves when we travel to a country or state that is new to us, so do we discover different dimensions of ourselves when we enter new terrain within consciousness. Declare that you are an adventurer in consciousness, traversing this three-dimensional realm to behold the wonders of creation. Then you will no longer be a passive tourist in your life. Search yourself and see how you move in the world. Do you delay or deny good in your life because you believe that an outer condition must first change? Have you put your life on pause while you wait for outer circumstances to shift before you become an adventurer, an explorer in consciousness? The world won't be any different once you press the play button if there is no corresponding change in your consciousness.

As a spiritual adventurer, include in your spiritual practice a willingness to stay on the razor's edge, not to become so comfortable that you become lethargic or mechanical in your spiritual practices. Consciousness is limitless, so you want to continue discovering deeper and deeper dimensions of your being. When you fully participate in life you courageously venture into unexplored territory, aspects of being you didn't know existed because you kept on settling, surviving, conducting life as usual, in a state of mediocrity. Be bold enough to step out without knowing how things will end up but trusting enough to break through the safety net you have created for yourself. Experience the proverbial hero's journey of venturing out, experiencing challenges, growing through and transcending them, and returning homeward transformed within.

Your confidence to become a spiritual warrior increases as you do something as simple as meet new people, learn a new skill, or open your life to new possibilities. By taking advantage of even small opportunities to explore an unexpressed dimension of your being, you will increase your courage and discipline to be an explorer of the expansive territory within yourself.

What are you willing to do today or this week that's risky? Is your heart risking anything? Is there some forgiveness that you need to initiate, amends you must make that you fear the other person will reject? Is there some generosity of the heart that you must express, yet you don't want to look foolish? What keeps nagging at you to take action that you keep holding back on, postponing? Don't wait. Participate, risk, and grow now. The longer you hide out in the attempt to remain safe, the more you become fearful, nervous, hesitant. You will not be present as a participant in birthing a new world, a world that very much wants and needs the contribution of your consciousness.

You are on a cosmic adventure. How would you move in this world if you really went for it, if you realized that you would never die, that you would never lose anything? Wouldn't you have the courage to free yourself from the tyranny of trends? Wouldn't you walk boldly, fearlessly sharing, radiating, being a creative agent for change in our world? You have the power to launch your adventure in this instant. Will you do it?

### Affirmation

*In this moment, I acknowledge my natural ability to enter a conscious state of beholding the ecstatic being that I am. For this was I created, and it is now a priority in my life. With the courage of a spiritual warrior, I enter my spiritual adventure armed with trust, openness of mind and heart, and surrender.*

## Embodiment

In this moment of quietude, this moment of devotion, this moment of resolve, I surrender. I let go of all that would inhibit my realization of my oneness with the Spirit. I allow myself to feel that I'm living, moving, and having my being in the divine presence. It's everywhere. It's everywhere. It's everywhere being itself. I now allow it to express in and through me, to be me, the real me.

I now arise from the mist of illusion and release all obstructions to a realization of my wholeness, my completeness. I release anything that would hinder, block, delay, or obstruct the divine from flowing through and as me right now. Just as electricity is invisible unless it's shining through a light bulb, God is everywhere now, becoming visible through my hands and feet, through my generosity, forgiveness, and love.

It is in this awareness that I throw myself wide open and become available to the spirit of God, the spirit of life, the spirit of love to transform my consciousness. I speak this word knowing that my life is a dynamic emanation of my Source. It is so activated within me that something wonderful is taking place. Something magnificent, something joy-filled, something peaceful, something resurrecting, something jubilant, something victorious is happening now. The strongholds of negativity and crystallized thought and habit patterns that have emerged from my ego's sense of separation have no more power over me. They are being dissolved right now, re-qualified, redeemed.

I am no longer subject to the tyranny of trends. It has no power over my discernment, my clarity. I am a full participant in divine order. The body of my affairs now takes on that shape. There is a fundamental order and harmony that now takes over my life. It doesn't need my help; it needs my permission to come through. It needs me to let it. As a spiritual warrior, I welcome divine order and confidently move into whatever is required to become my Authentic Self. This is the Me of me I yearn to know and express.

A freedom song sings through me now. It's a song of infinite potential and divine possibility. I am in league with pure Spirit in the conscious co-creation of my life and body of affairs. I am a distribution center of generosity, joy, love, forgiveness, and beauty. I was born free and now enter the depths of my soul to discover my ultimate freedom. It is done.

## Notes

1. Paramahansa Yogananda, *The Bhagavad Gita* (Los Angeles: Self-Realization Fellowship, 1995).
2. Ibid.
3. Ernest Holmes, *This Thing Called You* (New York: Penguin Group, 2004).
4. Osho, *Love, Freedom, and Aloneness: A New Vision of Relating* (New York: St. Martin's Press, 2001).
5. Genesis 1:31.
6. Genesis 3:6.
7. Numbers 14:18.

# 6
# Inner Ecology:
## Your Personal Laws of Life

*Trust love. Trust God that love*
*is everywhere, that we are here to be*
*perfect givers of love and receivers of love.*
*Love will have the final word.*

Our self-growth is fueled by the contents of our inner ecology. Our inner ecology is qualified by the personal laws of life by which we live. It's an illuminating, often startling, revelation to evaluate our personal laws of life. Whether or not you are aware that they are operable in your life, whether or not you have consciously explored them, they are the causality of the conditions and circumstances present in your life that determines your priorities, the quality of your relationships, finances, creative expression, physical well-being, and the spiritual path you do or do not follow. The state of mind in which you meet the circumstances in your life—be it laughter, tears, joy, fear, courage, integrity, generosity, creativity, confusion, clarity, acceptance, resistance, crazy thoughts, wise thoughts—is according to your personal laws of life.

In an open spirit of experimentation, you can discover right now the laws from which you self-express: Are you always talking about the past, speaking from your historical self, or from within the freshness of who you are in this moment? What are the contents of your conversations? Are they honest, genuine, guarded, open, loving, affirmative, uplifting, gossipy, complaining, critical? Are you living life on the layaway plan, spending some life-energy today and saving more to live for tomorrow? Or do you live each day full-out, withholding nothing from life? Your answers to these questions will provide insight into the mental habit patterns which comprise your laws of life.

## SETTING UNIVERSAL LAW IN MOTION

We live in an ever-evolving universe governed by cosmic law. Although universal law is impersonal in that it is not a respecter of persons and works for all alike, it becomes personalized through our individual application. Electricity, for example, operates by the same law no matter where, when, or by whom it is used. We don't step into a darkened room holding our breath as we switch on the light in hopes that electricity will work for us (unless we haven't paid our electric bill). We trust the law underpinning electricity.

There are many such laws governing the external world, and when society goes against them there are repercussions, such as our current experience with global warming. This is not the wrath of a God who sits in judgment and punishes us because we violated nature or some religious proscription. Universal law handles things when we are out of alignment with its principles. In just the same way, there are laws that govern the inner world of every individual. That which we call the external world and our individual, inner world are not separate. Universal law operates in both the visible and invisible realms. The entire web of life in all of its expressions is energetically intertwined; all that exists comes from the one Source, to which humanity has given many names and descriptions.

A practical purpose for deliberately exploring and experimenting with our personal laws of life is to discover how we apply them to accelerate or hinder our evolution. To see how this works, it may be helpful to begin with a common denominator with which we all must deal: money. Most individuals think that the bigger their bank balance the more affluent they are. Such a shortsighted understanding can cause people to be stingy, greedy, and to hoard out of fear of losing their money. Their energy only goes into how to invest, multiply, and above all, keep their money. They suffer from what is actually a type of poverty mentality. (Don't we all know people who have a lot of money yet remain inwardly poor?)

If an individual has only a monetary concept of affluence, then regardless of how much money they accumulate, it will never be enough. There is never enough of "more, more, more." As paradoxical as it may seem, having so much more than what we need becomes a statement of lack, not of having. However, when an individual's relationship to money includes sharing and circulating, the law of reciprocation is activated in such a way that money freely circulates back to them. Their bank balance may or may not equal that of a hoarder, but money will circulate freely throughout their life.

Living by the theme that "more is better" can cause a poverty mentality. Even if you live in a castle, that castle eventually becomes a cage. Affluence, or genuine wealth, includes the ability to discern the true meaning and place of monetary resources in one's life. The only concept of "more" that does not create a poverty mentality is being more of one's Authentic Self, thereby releasing more life-energy.

Taking our cue from nature, we can see that we live in an abundant universe. The same Cause of this abundance, through a creative act, has taken the form of each one of us. It has individualized itself as us. Because the Cause of the universe is abundant and we are made of the same substance, we too are predisposed to abundance. The law of abundance is activated when we realize that all of our needs are already met at every level of existence. In other words, we are not here to merely mope or cope. We are here to align our personal laws of life with the cosmic laws governing the universe and thereby flourish.

Those who believe that the source of affluence is the material realm are poor in spirit. Those who know that they are one with the Cause of existence are rich in spirit because they realize that, as they attune themselves with First Cause, their needs are met.

## MATURE AND IMMATURE WANTING

Wants and desires generate our aspirations, intentions, and motivations. Whether it's a luxury car or enlightenment, it's still a want, and every want vibrates at a specific energy level. Discernment allows us to understand the difference between the two types of wanting: mature wanting and immature wanting. Immature wanting originates in the surface mind and parrots, "I want this, I want that. I want, want, want." It's a "wanting to want" mind-set. Immaturity's mantra is "He who dies with the most toys wins." Immature wanting operates from the poverty mentality of "I don't have enough," even if one's worldly possessions are as high as a Himalayan peak. This mind-set of lack becomes individual personal law, leaving its practitioner hungry for the "more" that can only come from within, not from the external material world.

The mature level of wanting says, "I want to know more of who and what I really am. I want to express my true nature of love, joy, creativity, abundance, compassion, self-givingness, generosity. And this same good I desire for myself I desire for all beings." As you embrace this personal law of life, you align with the true nature of the universe, you tap into the rich reservoir of your innate wisdom. From this generative consciousness, your needs are met. The Hindu *Taittiriya Upanishad* tells us that, "He who realizes the sphere of space hidden in the cavern of his heart grasps all that may be desired and comes into contact with the Immensity."[1] To have a conscious realization of that Immensity is the desire that satisfies all desires. It is our true wealth.

## PHYSICAL SCIENCE IS NOW AFFIRMING WHAT SPIRITUAL SCIENCE HAS ALWAYS KNOWN

Quantum advancements in technological instruments are making it possible for scientific study to come closer to describing the "inner life" or consciousness within our universe. This causative consciousness is responsible for the course of the planets, the growth of a blade of grass, and the evolution of human beings. Sri Aurobindo, a towering figure and Vedic philosopher, wrote, "The true name of Causality is Divine Law, and the essence of that Law is an inevitable self-development."[2]

To make First Cause and its cosmic laws more approachable and friendly, the world's spiritual traditions use names and descriptions such as God, Brahma, Creator, Allah, Yahweh. People may not agree about the existence of a "God" according to literal concepts in traditional religions, but most people believe in the existence of love and intelligence. Actually, we could eliminate the word *God* from our vocabulary but not love or intelligence. In any case, the self-realized seers and sages endeavored to clothe in words their realizations of our Source as a way to convey the wisdom that the material comes from the nonmaterial.

For example, Zen Buddhism, a non-theism, teaches that emptiness is form, form is emptiness, meaning that all that is visible has come out of the invisible, that both are equally paradoxical when we endeavor to reduce them to solid concepts.

### EMBODYING A CONSCIOUSNESS OF LOVE

If you are curious to know if love has a major presence as a personal law of your life, observe how often you allow or block love from flowing in and out of your experience. Do you say, "Today I'm going to protect myself. I'm not going to get hurt," and then cloister your heart, blocking the energy of love that longs to be both a receiving and giving channel through your life? Or do you look for the countless ways in which life is eager to receive and reciprocate your gift of love?

You don't have to be in the headlines as a world philanthropist or feed millions of people. You can simply wish all the drivers on the freeway a safe journey, knowing that they, just like you, want to arrive safely at their destination. If you hear the sound of a fire engine or an ambulance, you can immediately broadcast a goodwill blessing from your heart for the welfare of all concerned. When listening to the news, you can immediately send healing energy out into the world. Throw yourself into life's current of Love-Intelligence and you will understand its highest meaning and make it one of your personal laws of life.

You may also apply this exercise to other qualities, such as creativity, happiness, generosity, and so on.

### SPIRITUAL MATURITY

A theme repeated throughout this book is that everything you need to fulfill your highest purpose on the planet is already within you. Whether it's been through the doctrine of original sin, education, family, or society, we have lost sight of our pristine essence, our essential propensity for enlightenment. The quantity and variety of spiritual and self-help books on the market today is a testimony to our collective desire to recapture what the Authentic Self already knows about us: we are unbounded potential waiting to be realized.

As we mature around our concept of the Godhead, we take responsibility for our lives. *We grow out of our childhood fantasies that there is a Great Something outside of us manipulating the environment, running the affairs of the universe by a reward-punishment system. We give up our status as a beggar and let God off the hook of being Santa Claus.* We recognize two kinds of laws operating in life: manmade prescriptive laws of do's and don'ts, such as don't drive over 65 miles per hour and do stop at a red light, and descriptive laws which describe the impersonal, lawful nature of the universe, such as water becomes ice when it reaches a certain temperature. As human beings, we live by both laws—that is the nature of our three-dimensional planet, heaven and earth joined together.

## WALKING ON THE RAZOR'S EDGE

During our earthly sojourn, we walk the razor's edge between our mortality and immortality. Mortality screams at us, "Please don't blow this incarnation! You have a very precious, sweet lifetime, so invite love, affluence, joy, and creativity to pour forth through you." Simultaneously, the voice of immortality encourages us to "Use your innate knowing that you are an eternal being to keep you free from ignorance, greed, and fear." *Walking this razor's edge of "don't blow this incarnation" and "you are an eternal being," we bounce back and forth as we learn to join heaven and earth without sacrificing one for the other. Our challenge is to eliminate the neuroses of a divided existence. As you spiritually mature, you make peace with the temporariness yet preciousness of your earthly incarnation, with the fact that you are here to bring Eternity into time.*

The human mind cannot contain, cannot wrap itself around the ultimate truths of existence because they are beyond the mind. As we mature, we reduce our insistence on having tidy answers to all of life's seeming paradoxes in order to feel more safe and secure. We trust in the fundamental goodness governing the universe. We relax in the mystery, grateful simply to know that at no moment in time are we separate from the Immensity that is the presiding, enlivening energy of all that there is.

## BE AT PEACE WITH YOUR EVOLVING CONSCIOUSNESS

A conscious realization of our innate oneness with the Ineffable does not mean that we will never make a mistake again. Even enlightened beings burn their bagels once in a while. It's important to maintain a sense of humor because this is how you will stop being afraid of making a mistake. You'll make some, but so what? That's why they're called mis-takes. Humor relaxes the uptight ego. You get a new cue from your inner Self and simply say, "I missed my cue, so let's do a second take." Your willingness to take the risk of making a mistake is actually an expression of courage and a willingness to grow from them. Mistakes are about getting the blessing in the lesson and the lesson in the blessing.

When your personal laws of life include walking in balance between the mortal and the immortal, you become confident, and confidence leads you to acknowledge your worthiness and to deliver your talents and gifts on the planet. *Walking the razor's edge of mortality and immortality keeps you finely tuned and sensitized to using your mortality to keep you honest about your incarnation, and your immortality to keep you aware of your true nature of oneness with Immensity.*

### YOU CAN'T DIVORCE YOURSELF

Consider using this introspective exercise often: You are the only person you can't divorce. For the eternity that lies before you, you are going to be with yourself. If you are going to be with yourself just the way you are in this moment, will you be happy? Can you live with yourself throughout eternity just the way you are? Let your answer be a guide to the laws of life and the qualities you want to cultivate and the mental habit patterns you wish to transform.

### CONTEMPLATING DEATH IS HEALTHY

I learned a lesson in sharpening the razor's edge a few years ago when I was purchasing life insurance. When the agent came to my office accessorized with his portable EKG machine, I thought little of it—after all, I follow a vigorous daily exercise routine and enjoy excellent health. Imagine my surprise when, following the test, he announced that I had advanced heart disease. I contested with, "I'm feeling too good to have anything wrong with me!" Of course, he thought I was just in denial so insisted on returning with a replacement machine to retest me. On this second visit, he said not only did I have heart disease, it was unclear how much longer I'd be on the planet. He supported his diagnosis saying, "I've been in the insurance business for many years. I don't want to upset you, but it appears you are going to die." I replied, "Yes, but not today." I then went to a cardiologist who, after a battery of tests, pronounced my heart as healthy.

The time between the insurance agent telling me that I was going to die, and the cardiologist saying my heart was healthy, gave me pause to reflect that one day I am indeed going to die. I used this acceptance to determine how I was going to live the rest of my life. It gave me cause to consider what I wanted to clean up in this lifetime and how I could make the best use of the rest of this incarnation. The razor's edge instantly became very sharp, offering me a potent motive for examining my personal laws of life.

Most of us have had an occasion in life that positioned us on the razor's edge. Whether its been long ago or recent, go back to a time when you were on the spot, pressed against the ropes, and recapture not the fear but the sharp sense of urgency, of immediacy you felt. An incarnation is very brief, and our inner awakening is of the ultimate urgency. Use the razor's edge to motivate yourself to become free and end the cycle of suffering.

## PRACTICE, PRACTICE, PRACTICE

That which transforms your life is what you *practice*. And what you practice constitutes your personal laws of life—not what you merely believe in, but what you *practice*. It's all well and good to read book, and to attend seminars, lectures, and workshops, and to say, "Oh, that really resonates with me! It's now part of my life's philosophy." Your philosophy may give you a temporary state of euphoria, but if you want to be anchored in Reality, it takes practice, practice, practice. We are not here to be euphoric but to get free. *Rudimentary spirituality is theory; advanced spirituality is practice*. What you practice, you ultimately embody, paving the way for breakthroughs, insights, fresh realizations, and the evolution of consciousness. In truth, that which is inconceivable is caught and understood by those who are making their spiritual practices a way of life.

Wise are they who devote their lives to evolutionary inner practices. Why not make it a sacred, vital, juicy happening? **First**, sit to meditate on a daily basis, preferably first thing in the morning. Experiment with various techniques of meditation that are readily available and find the one that suits your temperament. To guide you in selecting a technique, an important question to ask is, "What is my purpose for beginning a meditation practice?" Your answer will guide you to a method suited to your purpose. Then, after some experimentation ask, "Is it working?"

Even if it's just for ten minutes a day, sit in the stillness practicing your technique. I encourage you to practice a silent rather than guided (spoken word) meditation because it is silence that will lead you into profound stillness, and it is stillness that attunes you to the still, small voice of intuitive guidance.

**Second**, consciously circulate life-energy in the world, which means expressing kindness, encouragement, compassion, and sharing of your financial resources. What you circulate returns to you; that's what a circuit is—that which returns to its point of origin. You get to keep that which you give away. This cosmic law of circulation is taking place throughout the Universe. Are you circulating or stagnating? Are you circulating love, generosity, peace? Ask yourself where you consistently give of yourself and where you withhold yourself from life.

Generosity is a vital law of life, and the joy of giving has its own enriching rewards. When you are charitable—which means having a generous heart—you are a giver. Stealth-giving, or giving anonymously, is a beautiful practice. Find places where you can give to someone without allowing yourself to be caught doing it. You know someone needs money, so you slip some into an envelope and let them "find" it. There are other forms of giving, such as supporting your spiritual community and humanitarian organizations. Through all forms of giving, you become a vehicle through which the Spirit gives of itself. When you train yourself to be in the flow of affluence through generosity of the heart, you align yourself with the givingness of the universe, transforming the world in which you live. You become a beneficial presence on the planet.

**Third**, as you celebrate the flow of Goodness into your life, celebrate the good that flows into the lives of others as though it were your own. Giving thanks for the good that happens to a friend, co-worker, family member, and especially a seeming enemy as though it has happened to you is a spiritual practice that breaks down a sense of competition, separation, and the belief that there is not enough good to go around. It eases the pangs of envy that we sometimes experience and takes the edge off of an attitude that says, "When am I going to get mine?" If we are honest, we will see that sometimes we walk around with that kind of despair, that kind of attitude in our consciousness which only serves to block the flow of good available to us. When we break the stranglehold of such a mind-set, we step back into the flow of gratitude and open ourselves to an even greater influx of good.

You are predisposed to vibrant health, affluence, love, compassion, creativity, generosity, equanimity, kindness—high octane qualities that will reconfigure your life in such a way that you will have tangible evidence that you are on the planet for a purpose. You have all that you need to live a fulfilling, dynamic, creative life. Why settle for less than what you are meant to experience? As Sri Aurobindo so aptly put it, "In all spiritual living the inner life is the thing of first importance . . . God-love and the delight of God will be the heart's expression of inner communion and oneness, and that delight and love will expand itself to embrace all existence."[3] What a spiritually efficient way to live!

### Affirmation

*Today, as I enter my meditation practice, I am open and receptive to my inner spirit revealing to me the personal laws of life by which I live. I courageously look at myself in all honesty and with full confidence in my ability to co-create with the Spirit the life I am here to live.*

### Embodiment

Right here and right now, I enter the Spirit's full dimension of unconditional love, peace, clarity. In the light of this clarity, I align my awareness with universal law. My entire inner being opens and welcomes these qualities as my laws of life.

I fully accept that abundance is a natural by-product of the law of circulation. How good it is to know that it is a natural part of my being. I think from this place, I act from this place, and I express generosity of heart. I share my resources knowing absolutely that the source and substance of my supply is limitless. Oh, how magnificently practical it is to live from this realization. I know that abundance is a law of life, and I radiate the manifestation of all needs met for all beings.

I live in the secret place of the Most High, of First Cause, my Source. With my feet firmly planted on the earth and my heart directed heavenward, my inner ecology is enlivened, upleveled, and grounded. The universal laws by which I navigate my life are fully revealed to me. I gratefully acknowledge those areas in which I have yet to grow. I welcome them. I embrace them. With full confidence, I recognize that all which I need in order to shift and transform my consciousness is within me. I see also those areas in which the Spirit works through me, and I humbly give thanks.

I now tap the reservoir of the ever-expanding realm of the Spirit and unify with this presence. From this Source comes the whole of existence—that which is called good and that which is called bad. In divine mind, no such distinctions exist, and they now cease to exist in my mind. Life exists, life in all of its expressions. How beautiful it is when one has the inner eyes to see with clarity. How precious is this human incarnation.

I accept full responsibility for my life with grace and ease, knowing that it is a divine expression, that I am an individualized expression of my beloved God, the joy, the life that is everywhere present. In this Presence, I know that it is not possible for me to blow my incarnation because my intention to awaken is sincere. I forgive myself for the missteps along the path because I realize that they are inevitable in all stages of growth. I honor, respect, and accept myself. And just as I extend compassion to myself in my process of growth, so do I have compassion for others. Just as I make room in my heart for myself, so do I make room for my brothers and sisters on the planet.

The laws of my life are those of harmony, generosity, peace, wisdom, compassion, and service. I declare this to be the landscape of my inner ecology, and I give thanks for it. In this space, there is room for all that I am, including that which awaits the transforming touch of my spiritual discernment and commitment to transform.

As I sit in the stillness of the Self, my breathing and heart rate slow down. My digestive system relaxes. My entire body is in harmony with wholeness. I live, move, and have my being in it. I fully enter this vortex of surrender and swim in the sea of divine support, empowerment, transforming knowledge, and divine love. I walk on the water of this consciousness. In the mirror of my meditation I see my original face, my inherent beauty and goodness. How sweet. How tender. How vulnerable I am to the Spirit.

This word that I speak does not fight or contend with any secondary causative factor. It does not contend with the past or future. It embraces this now moment of awareness. I break free from the illusory factor of this world and step into the luminosity of divine understanding. I accept and claim that all of my needs are met by the Infinite, the all good of God announcing itself within my life, as my life. This is the law of life in which I live, move, and have my being, and I humbly give thanks for it.

## Notes

1. Alain Daniélou, *Taittiriya Upanishad, The Gods of India* (New York: Inner Traditions International, Ltd., 1985).
2. Aurobindo Ghose, *The Life Divine* (Twin Lakes, Wisc.: Lotus Light Publications, 1949).
3. Ibid.

# 7
# Energetic Shapeshifting:
## A Practical Practice for Urban Shamans

*The songs of all my great-grandmothers*
*And the dreams of all my great-grandfathers*
*The dance of heaven and earth*
*All live in me, all live in me*

In the mysterious pageant of our lives, some aspects of our life-structures function at a high level of satisfaction and others, in spite of our best efforts to transform them, seem as though they have a shelf life that will outlast our own. Sometimes the desired transformation of a life-pattern hasn't come about because we haven't yet encountered a practice tailored to its distinct characteristics. The spiritual path is not a "one-size-fits-all" solution to either the small or super-sized challenges we face, just as no one teaching or teacher has a monopoly on the truth.

A variety of paths and practices exists to suit different temperaments, levels of consciousness, awareness, and adeptness of practice. We may follow one or several paths over the course of our lives determined by pivotally timed alignments in our evolutionary process. We may be inspired to practice a meditation technique from one path, a form of ritual from another, chanting or prayer from yet a different one, and practices for cultivating skillful means to work with our neurotic tendencies from others. It is in this spirit that I offer you the practice of energetic shapeshifting for navigating the inner and outer terrain of consciousness.

## ENERGY: THE BASIC COMPONENT OF LIFE

Before we launch into the practice of shapeshifting and its practical application to the challenges of twenty-first-century living, it is important to understand what shapeshifting is not. Shapeshifting is not action based on superstition, pushing our willful agenda, or manipulating people or conditions.

The West, unfortunately, has a history of taking profound spiritual teachings—especially from other cultures—and diluting, glamorizing, romanticizing, and commercializing them into moneymakers. Shamanism and shapeshifting, in some cases, have been reduced to a colorful deck of power-animal cards and vision quests conducted at five-star hotels. (The same has been done with the ancient Hindu *tantric* teachings, which in Western society resembles nothing like the practice of the original tantrics which took place in crematory grounds without 600-thread-count sheets. However, how an individual enters their spiritual practice is a sacred act.)

In stark contrast to the spiritual pop model, it is encouraging to know that many Westerners have studied with shamans of all cultures. One such individual is John Perkins, who apprenticed with indigenous Shuar of the Amazon in 1968. Today, John shares shamanic wisdom about how the visible world is governed by invisible energetic laws that are operable from the rainforests to corporate boardrooms. His clientele has grown to include corporate executives from all types of businesses. They learn from him how an urban shaman may serve the Spirit, the individual, as well as the local and global communities. Individuals from all walks of life support his Dream Change Coalition, an organization dedicated to environmental, economic, and social change.

The fundamental principle in shapeshifting is the realization that life is made up of energy. Everything that is alive requires energetic life force in order to exist. As the Mayan healer-shaman Vieja Itza said to John Perkins, "Energy. It is everything. We are energy. That is all there is to it. The shapeshifter believes she can influence her relationship with the physical world. Therefore, she can. Belief… and one thing more. Intent."[1] Through his description we can outline the inner process of the shapeshifter. *First: the acceptance that energy is the cosmic building block and sustainer of all that exists. Second: the conviction that an individual may energetically influence his or her inner and outer world. Third: navigating energy through one's intent is the action necessary to shapeshift and bring about the desired transformation.*

Energetic shapeshifting is one of the world's oldest traditions of healing and transformation. It occurs in two forms: spiritual shapeshifting, which transforms or reshapes the conditions of one's consciousness and life, and shifting one's actual physical shape, such as a shaman assuming the body of a jaguar, or a form of nature.

### A DAY IN THE LIFE OF A SHAMAN

Although I had read about shamans from cultures as diverse as Siberia, Alaska, China, Egypt, and others, this did not prepare me for the impact of my personal encounter with Baba when, in 1998, I conducted a pilgrimage to the West African country of Ghana.

My group and I visited an indigenous people who had not been affected by Christian missionaries, which enabled them to preserve their shamanic practices. Shamans within the community were able to shapeshift into whatever was needed under any circumstance, whether it required taking on the energetic shape of an animal or an element in nature.

Soon after our arrival, a young boy approached me and said, "Baba is waiting for you."

"Baba?" I thought I must have heard wrong.

My interrogator authoritatively responded with another question, "Are you the teacher from California?"

I nodded to the affirmative and was informed that Baba was considered a powerful shaman to whom thousands flocked seeking a panacea for their physical ailments and heartaches. My young escort asked me to go with him alone, without my group. We took a taxi until we reached the edge of the jungle. From that point on, we could only go on foot into the thickets. We walked together in silence until we reached a modest hut with many people standing and sitting around waiting for their turn to see Baba. Baba, I learned, was in his eighties, and his father, who was a healer in another village, was 134!

After a few minutes of being the object of curious though friendly stares, I was approached by Baba's apprentice who led me to a waiting room from which I could see Baba working with a woman. When I asked the apprentice what Baba was doing, he said that the woman wanted to remarry. Although she was already married to two other men, they no longer lived in her village and the desire of her heart was to set up life with someone local. Baba was working to free her energy ties from her previous two husbands. Once freed, she would then be able to "see" the energy of the man she was to marry.

Unknown to me, my turn was next. I was sure there was an appropriate protocol for greeting Baba, and as I made my feeble attempt he noticed that I was limping. All at once Baba began speaking in his native language motioning wildly with his hands, causing everyone who was in the waiting room to laugh uproariously. As it turned out, in his shamanic vision, he saw that I had made five shots into a basketball hoop and, when I went up for the sixth shot, I had ruptured my Achilles tendon. Through a translator, Baba indicated that it was a spiritual injury representing the jealousy of enemies, but that it was not necessary for me to be concerned because I was protected. He went on to say that I was now ready for my next ring of power, which required that I spend the next three days with him in the bush.

I respectfully explained that I was responsible for an entire pilgrimage group and that I couldn't abandon them, which caused another burst of collective laughter from the waiting room. Baba broke it down for me saying, "I sent for you months ago." My only possible response was silent agreement. I then excused myself saying that I had to inform my group, who were waiting for me back at the village. Upon my arrival, I found everyone intermingling with the villagers and laughing, talking, and listening to stories about ancestors. When I told them I wouldn't be back at the hotel in time for evening dinner, they responded to my pending adventure with a "There he goes again, being himself" smile of generosity and acceptance.

It was dark by the time I returned to Baba's village. I had lost all track of time, which was fine since it had no relevance in Baba's reality. Baba gestured to some of his apprentices that they were to accompany us into the jungle. These men were briskly walking in the darkest dark I had ever experienced, never bumping into a tree or tripping over branches. Their vision did not divide the day into the night, light into dark—it was all the same to them. I, on the other hand, struggled to keep pace with them, hampered by my lack of their night vision, tripping over things that make their home on the jungle floor. The noises made by jungle night prowlers and hunters was piercing to the core, but my enthusiasm for this unique adventure overrode their influence.

As we continued walking toward our destination, Baba began to chant. As though out of nowhere, a voice that didn't belong to anyone in the group began to answer. Baba stopped abruptly and turned in the direction of the voice. From my vantage point, I watched him shapeshift into a womanly countenance. In a gentle yet directive voice he said, "English," and gestured for me to approach him. "My older brother Tree will speak now," Baba said. It was then that I realized the voice was actually coming from a tree, a tree that addressed me in perfect English asking, "Are you the teacher from California?"

Transfixed, I simply said, "Yes." The tree-shaman began speaking to me about my spiritual community, Agape, and prophesied that I was going to be actively involved with harbingers of the world's peace and peace programs. After advising me on other personal matters—I didn't even have to ask questions—my new brother Tree comforted me by saying that I was protected and guided, a repetition of Baba's earlier statement.

On our return walk to Baba's hut, it appeared to be daybreak, even though I knew it was still dark. The jungle floor, which I experienced as total darkness during our trek into its interior, was now luminous, lit by the same light that Baba and his apprentices saw. In addition to seeming magical, it was also practical because I no longer held up the others with my constant tripping.

When we arrived back at Baba's, he said that because of my sobriety and lack of fear around the brother Tree that I did not have to stay for three days, that the purpose for which he called me had been fully realized. I understood that the gift I had just received was not mine alone—it was a transmission from another dimension of life that was to be shared with my entire community and beyond. To have read about shamanic shapeshifting was one thing. To have been in the presence of Baba, to have seen his tribesmen walk through a jungle that was lighted by their altered vision and to have heard the mellifluous voice of brother Tree was quite another. I still consider it one of those extraordinary blessings of a lifetime.

## SHAPESHIFTING: AN INTENTIONAL ACT OF TRANSFORMATION

If you are willing to do the inner work required, you are ripe for shapeshifting, which is a synonym for transformation. Maybe you're already saying, "Great. I know exactly what I intend to transform, so let's get on with it." But simply identifying your intention is not the whole deal. As it relates to energy and intention, shapeshifting is a highly disciplined, inside job that requires cutting through the illusion of ourselves as being solid entities, the thickness of our restlessness, our mental business and speediness. We must identify and purify our motivations for what it is that we wish to shapeshift.

African and Native American shamans go into what is called the dream state, an altered, mystical state of interiorized consciousness. Chinese Taoist shapeshifters use meditation, dancing, singing, chanting, ritual—activities that usher them into an awareness of oneness with life. We urban shamans must also set the proper inner and outer atmosphere for practicing the sacred art of shapeshifting by entering into communion with our Spirit Self, that about us which is formless.

You may begin by selecting an indoor or outdoor space conducive to gathering your energy and centering yourself. Plan to allow a minimum of twenty to thirty minutes for your first session. The following instructions are a meditative, centering preparation for shapeshifting.

Sitting in a firm chair or on a floor cushion, assume a posture of power by sitting with your back straight, a few inches away from the back of the chair. Rest your palms, turned upward or downward, on your thighs, and place your feet flat on the floor. If you're sitting on a floor cushion, sit with your legs crossed and buttocks supported with extra pillows so that your hips are higher than your knees for proper back support. Your eyes may be open or closed. You may find it helpful to close your eyes and gently place your focus at the third eye, which is located in the middle of the forehead at the point just above the eyebrows. To center yourself, become aware of your breath by mentally following your inhalations and exhalations without controlling them—just breathe naturally.

Begin to contemplate your oneness with life's Source and how all beings are interconnected to one another, to the animal kingdom, to the mineral kingdom, to all of Mother Earth. Continue in this recognition for about five to ten more minutes.

Once you feel centered, bring your intention into your awareness. Hold your awareness in an open and receptive state. Don't be frustrated by the discursiveness of your thoughts, which are quite normal to meditators regardless of their mileage on the cushion. Imagine your thoughts as clouds in the sky, just floating by without leaving an imprint, which is how not to get hooked and carried off by them.

Gently begin to examine the motives underlying your intention. Once you are clear about them, you are ready to energize your intention. State your intent verbally or silently. Whichever you choose, suffuse it with the energy of your conviction that you are not speaking into a void but into a universal law that responds to the energy of your word.

Then, simply rest; let go into the energy you have established. You may continue to watch your breath and remain in the silence.

When you bring your session to a close, give thanks in the language of your heart.

I emphasize how important it is to examine the motives of your intent. If you want to shapeshift from driving a Mini Cooper into a Hummer, well, it's not exactly a crime. However, understand that your *unconscious motives* carry an energy frequency that also impacts the shapeshifting process. You may think you want a 242-horsepower vehicle, but is what you really desire a sense of personal power? If so, let your intention be to shapeshift into an embodiment of personal power rather than an external symbol of it. Discerning your more subtle motives will guide you to the genuine desires of your heart.

#### SHAPESHIFTING IN THE MIDST OF THE UNEXPECTED

I recently had a crash course for shapeshifting on the physical level when I was out walking my dog, Sheba. From seemingly out of nowhere, another dog lunged at Sheba and a fight broke out. I automatically jumped into the fray to protect the dogs from each other. My adrenaline was flowing so strongly I lost all bodily awareness while exerting myself in successfully separating them. I continued walking down the street, grateful that neither dog was hurt, when suddenly I noticed blood on my right shoe. I rolled up my pant leg and, sure enough, there was a deep gash in my knee. As I limped my way home, my experiences with the shamans in West Africa burst into my awareness like a mystical directive reminding me to practice the gift I had received from them.

I began immediately. However, in my zeal, I started backwards. I caught myself, refocused my intent, and shapeshifted the energy from my healthy left knee over to my injured right knee. Attuning myself to the wholeness in my left knee, I accepted that same experience for my right knee as I continued to navigate the energy of wholeness into it. I contemplated how the entire body is an organized whole with every organ and part interdependent upon the other, just as the universe is an organized whole. By the time I reached my front door, my knee had stopped bleeding and the throbbing was greatly reduced. The rest I was able to handle with a good-sized bandage.

I learned from this that even under the most unexpected, spontaneous circumstances, it is possible to shapeshift through the power of intention. While the meditative approach is a deliberate setting aside of time to shapeshift, once you have some practice, you can experiment with shapeshifting on a bus, in the elevator, anywhere you can comfortably gather your energies and focus yourself on the practice.

### BECAUSE YOU GIVE IT ENERGY, IT EXISTS

Where we invest our energy is a result of choice. No one outside of us forces us to invest our energy in any particular emotion, thought, or act. The energy investment choices we make are either conscious or unconscious. Either way, where we direct the energy of our thoughts and emotions gives rise to our experiences.

Unconscious shapeshifting occurs during the most ordinary, everyday activities. Say a friend calls you on the phone and asks how you're doing. "Oh, my back hurts," you respond. Or, when someone asks what's going on in your life you say, "I don't know how I'm going to pay my mortgage." These responses drain your energy. Or let's say you start recounting something negative that happened to you ten years ago. What you are doing is energetically shapeshifting by bringing your past into your present, along with its negative energy. Now there's nothing wrong with informing someone about what ails you, but it's the state of consciousness in which you do so that makes all the difference. If you are unconscious, then you don't take self-responsibility, so all that's left to do about your situation is to play the victim and complain to anyone who has the patience to listen.

In contrast, when you are conscious, you are aware of how the laws of the universe work. This positions you to take self-responsibility for the conditions present in your life as well as for your healing and transformation. Then, when you share with a confidante something you are going through or have experienced in the past, you are not speaking from a disempowered or negative state of consciousness. You reveal what you have learned or are still learning from your experiences that vitalize your life and evolve your consciousness.

Do you sense the difference between vibrating at a rate of energy on the affirmative level compared to the negative level? Being affirmative is not about going into a state of denial about life's challenges. *It's about focusing your intent on what you want to occur rather than on what you don't want to occur*. When you are negatively attuned to your desired transformation, you end up developing coping mechanisms or defense mechanisms to justify a particular habit pattern. You learn "to live with it," when you have all the power you need to shapeshift it. Becoming more conscious is vital to our sense of well-being and empowers us to fully know ourselves.

## AT PLAY IN THE FIELD OF COSMIC ENERGY

As you begin to understand what it means to play in a unified field of energy, shapeshifting becomes a powerful gateway into this rarefied atmosphere. To understand energy is to know why and how shapeshifting works. *The reason shapeshifting works so efficiently is because all we are ever dealing with is energy*. Here's an exercise that you may use to sensitize and recalibrate your spiritual nervous system to become receptive to shapeshifting.

Begin by taking a long, slow inhalation followed by a long, slow exhalation. Next, bring into awareness an area of your life that is in alignment with harmony, wholeness—even if it's something as simple as being able to take a deep breath. The point of this step is to break free, even for a few minutes, from thoughts about your life challenges.

Next, drop the label you have placed on the harmonious area of your life. Simply rest in the energy of harmony itself, without naming it. Hang out in this energetic essence for a few moments.

Then, bring into your awareness an aspect of your life that you feel is inharmonious. Become fully present to it without judgment or spinning off into any opinions you may have about it. Stop and reconnect to the energy of harmony. Shapeshift this harmonious energy into the aspect of your life you wish to imbue with harmony and wholeness. Do this, without over-trying, as many times as you feel necessary. Accept that you may enter and play in this energy field whenever you want. Bring your play-practice to a close by giving thanks for the experience, blessing yourself and all beings.

With enough practice, you will realize that you are not thinking, feeling, and acting with energy, but *from* energy. Then, you will understand why you can consciously co-create through universal law a life lived in harmony, peace, joy, creativity. You will be like Albert Einstein who, when he discovered his theory of relativity, was in what could be described as a shamanic, dreamlike state. He saw himself riding a beam of light throughout creation. According to his description, he was traveling at the speed of light, and when he reentered the waking state, he wrote the theory of relativity. It's interesting to think about what he would have come up with had he continued his shamanic ride—perhaps a theory of "unitivity." (*Unitivity* is one of my coined expressions.

I rhymed *relativity*—in case a rapper wants to take it all home.) Einstein might have discovered that the light wasn't traveling at all, that it was both the journey and the destination.

This is the truth of our own nature—we travel the path of awakening only to discover that we have been enlightened all along.

## PITFALLS ON THE PATH

Much of the time when we could be sitting in meditation or shapeshifting, we create excuses not to do so. Cleaning our closet or other tasks suddenly take on an urgency over our spiritual practices. We're all familiar with the well-worn excuses we use to rationalize neglecting our spiritual practices. If you have a certain amount of spiritual mileage, you are, by now, becoming a connoisseur of your neuroses and the excuses they justify, which gives you an edge in transcending them.

Another pitfall to avoid on your journey is the ego's delay system, which shows up in the form of "I don't know what to do. Now what do I do? What do you think I should do?" In such a state, you've entered the energy frequency of procrastination, which will only keep you going in circles. Such thought forms are mental units of energy invested in conscious or unconscious fear. You have a method for finding out what to do: introspective contemplation. Nothing stands against you other than your own limited view, your limited opinions, your limited perceptions of yourself, your personal laws of life that have condensed into your experiences, your life circumstances. By shapeshifting from relativity to unitivity, you will discover that your progress is not determined by heredity or karma. Your cosmic destiny as an enlightened being and the commitment with which you remove the obstacles to realizing your naturally awakened state of consciousness are the determinants of your progress.

**CRAZY-SANITY: OXYMORON OR SYNONYM?**

Crazy-sanity is not an oxymoron. It is a state of consciousness that has been attributed to many awakened beings who have little in common with the values, goals, and accomplishments set by societal or worldly standards. In our postmodern society, you have to be at least a little crazy to not totally capitulate to its standards of material success. Oftentimes, it has been individuals who have stepped out of the mainstream who have contributed to the creation of a just and kind society. For example, when you look at the lives of Martin Luther King Jr., Mohandas K. Gandhi, and Mother Teresa, their respective visions seemed crazy in their time. But that didn't stop them from navigating the power of their intention into their visions and taking action. They were genuine lovers of humanity. So empowered were they in their giving and forgiving, kindness, and generosity of heart that they shapeshifted the energy of hatred, prejudice, and separation into love, compassion, and oneness. The next stage of human evolution spoke itself through them as it does through individuals such as Nelson Mandela, Dr. A. T. Ariyaratne, and His Holiness the Dalai Lama. Theirs is not an exclusive club—we are all potential members!

We are at a stage in our collective evolution where we may transform ourselves and release from within us the sweet music of unconditional love, soul-confidence, and full-dimensional living. This means that, should you choose it, you may be crazy-sane: sane with love of the Spirit, crazy in love with life, sane with your realization of oneness with the Spirit of Life, all beings, all creatures. When you energetically shapeshift and transform limitation into expansion, you exercise the dominion that has been given to you. Spirit is waking up as itself in you. Life is for you, love is for you, abundance is for you, joy is for you, as are bliss, creativity, and elegance of being. Will you give your consent to consciously being for yourself?

## SHAPESHIFTING: REMOVER OF OBSTACLES

Most people live in a world of cognitive deficiency—"What you see is what you get." Life as it is described in newspapers and tabloids, on television, and in movies is thought to be "reality." That is backwards. Instead of individuals being taught that they are here to be co-creative agents of infinite possibilities, they are hypnotized into lives of limitation directed by societal systems and what the five senses can perceive. When we look out at what is "normal," we see the stockpiling of nuclear weapons, we hear politicians singing, "Bomb, bomb, bomb Iran." Others join in and move through life in a hypnotic trance of conformity. They think of themselves as supreme consumers; their mantra is "I am a consummate consumer here to buy, buy, buy." Their temple is the local mall and their intention is to accelerate their purchasing power. This is the shadow side of reality, a world that has far less light than the luminous Reality that expresses itself throughout every corner of the cosmos.

When your steps in life are ordered by a deliberate intention to evolve in consciousness, you energetically synchronize with your intention. Your visionary powers shift and reveal areas where you may be of service in the world. Rather than offering your love to get something in return, you love without agenda. You break free of the deal-making form of 50/50 love, "I'll love you if you love me; I'll give you this if you give me that," which is a relationship based on bargaining. Instead, you offer agenda-less love, love for no reason other than the joy of loving.

Shapeshifting neutralizes the lies we tell ourselves about life: that there is scarcity, not enough to go around, that if the stock market crashes so will your life because you are dependent upon the outer world rather your own consciousness. Shapeshifting re-grooves these energetic patterns of thought. Nothing dies—it only shapeshifts in form.

Begin now and join the ranks of shapeshifters who have gathered enough wisdom to become a beneficial presence on the planet. Oneness will be the order of your days. What an enlightened way to live.

### Affirmation

*As I interiorize my attention, I attune my energies with my inention to drop habits that distract me from my spiritual practice. I declare that I am prepared in consciousness to shapeshift, to transform, and to purify my motives and reduce them to one: self-realization. The universe supports me in my aspiration, and I express my gratitude by remaining true to my intention.*

### Embodiment

How wonderful and divine and perfect is the Spirit. How sacred is its presence expressing in, through, and as me. Appreciation wells up within me and breaks open my heart. From this inward glance I make myself available to seeing the Reality that has no name, no form. I sense and know the energy of its presence, and I know that it is here with me now, beating my heart, breathing my breath, perfectly functioning in my body, mind, and spirit. In this awareness, I accept my liberation right now. Now. Not tomorrow, but now.

In this now, I speak and embrace the spiritual idea that I live in the land of plentitude in all aspects of my life. Where thoughtforms of lack and scarcity have invaded my consciousness, I shapeshift them into abundance. I shapeshift my consciousness into the heavenly realm of ever-expanding good.

Where there were once concerns about health, I shapeshift them into a realization that I am whole, perfect, and complete. Every organ functions as it was created to support the body temple.

Any residue of anger, animosity, and resentment is now shapeshifted into compassion, lovingkindness, and forgiveness, both for myself and others. Generosity of the heart expresses freely and lavishly through me. I see my relationships filled with an energy of purpose and of spiritual growth.

Creativity freely flows through me as an expression of my talents, gifts, and skills. Oh, I know that they are used in a meaningful way to uplift, encourage, inspire, and comfort all with whom I come in contact. Any agreements that I have consciously or unconsciously made with mediocrity are now broken. I have shapeshifted my point of view, I have expanded my reference points from the little ego to the cosmic Self. I now walk hand-in-hand with excellence. I welcome the deeper dimensions of consciousness into my being as I participate in full-dimensional living.

With the realization that everything is energy, I see its glow everywhere I look, manifesting in all that I see. I know this to be the life force within all existence—every plant, animal, the creatures of the sea, mountains, rocks, even dirt. There is nothing that is not made of the energetic essence of the Spirit of life. It is my very being and nature of my Self. I am one with this Presence, and it reveals to me the next level of my ever-evolving consciousness. Any blockages that heretofore prevented me from realizing the truth of my being are dissolved in my communion with my Source, the Source of all that is.

Just as life holds back nothing from me, I hold back nothing from life. I am so grateful for my precious human incarnation, for the opportunity to realize what it is to harmonize body, mind, and spirit, to join heaven and earth. I know myself to be a lover of humanity, of my family, friends, and seeming enemies because I know they are all a manifestation of the Spirit.

And so it is with a full heart that I say thank you. Thank you Life, thank you pure Spirit for your unconditional love, compassion, and tenderness that is lavished upon me.

In this consciousness of gratitude I speak my intention to shapeshift into that person who is fully myself.

I now see the love of God flowing throughout all of my relationships. The world sings back to me now. The world reflects back to me now, "Oh, there you are. There you are, I've been looking for you. I've been wanting to express through you, you genius, you. I've been waiting for you to wake up, you genius. I've been waiting for you to wake up, you lover, you. I've been waiting for you to wake up, you expresser of love and joy. You are My beloved in whom I am well pleased. I get to express through you."

## Note

1. John Perkins, *Shapeshifting: Shamanic Techniques for Global and Personal Transformation* (Rochester, Vt.: Destiny Books, 1997).

# 8
# CREATIVELY MALADJUSTED

*The years on a road so narrow and long*
*Taught me to listen to life's sacred song*
*Can't you hear it?*

Are you ready to unleash your inner Don Quixote to "reach the unreachable star" and "live the impossible dream"? As you allow such a possibility to take root in your consciousness, your agreements with mediocrity will begin to dissolve and you will enter the evolutionary process of becoming creatively maladjusted.

You may say, "I'm not quite convinced that's for me. I've spent a lot of money and time in therapy to get *adjusted*. I'm not sure I'm ready to throw all of that painstaking effort away so I can now become creatively maladjusted—whatever that means anyway!"

Good. Question it, because once you enter a state of creative maladjustment, you can no longer fit back into the small space of existence you once occupied. But you can rely on the fact that living creatively maladjusted is beautiful because it creates space for you to be transformed by the moment-by-moment renewing of your mind, heart, and spirit. And since those who have made an impact for the better upon our world were creative nonconformists, you will be in good company.

### HOW TO FAIL SUCCESSFULLY

There's no escaping that today's definition of success has to do with celebrity—whether it's positive or negative doesn't matter, as long as it's about being known for something. Pause at the grocery checkout long enough to scan the tabloid headlines and you'll learn where and what celebrities are eating for lunch—"Oh, God, don't tell me she ate a ham sandwich! Why just last week she was protecting the rights of slaughterhouse animals." If the paparazzi is tailing you, you must be socially relevant.

As an example of just how neurotic segments of society have become, I read an article about people who have so projected their personality values on their pets that they buy fake testicles for their neutered dogs so that they will "look normal to other dogs." The inventor has sold 200,000 pairs to date! Now I love dogs and have two myself, but I don't think I'll rush out to buy testicles for them or have their teeth whitened or capped, which are also now popular pet grooming practices. At the Agape International Spiritual Center, we have a pet bereavement support group and conduct an annual animal blessing, but my spiritual community's resources will not be used for buying pets testicles as long as the world's children need financial support for healing their cleft palates.

When you're creatively maladjusted, you don't buy into the prevailing hot trends or the false belief that celebrity and success are synonymous. As a creative nonconformist, you don't fit so comfortably into our high-tech low-touch society, a society that spends more on bombs and weaponry than on taking care of people, that exalts personality and downplays character. Being creatively maladjusted in a society that values materialism over evolution of character is the higher part of wisdom.

Once you step out of living in the world depicted in the media, you break free of its mesmerism and are introduced to the possibility of creating a world that works for everyone, governed by the benevolent Love-Intelligence that is everywhere in its fullness.

## PERSONALITY VERSUS CHARACTER

Understand that to be creatively maladjusted is to know the vital distinction between personality and character. The word *character* is from the Old French *caractere* and means "imprint on the soul." The etymology of *personality* suggests veneer and is connected with the Latin word *persona*, which was a mask worn by actors. Character is revealed when our mask is removed.

It's easy to tell if you are living from character or personality: If things aren't going your way, personality pouts while character remains unruffled and learns from the experience. When you are not in psychologically or emotionally safe territory, personality panics. Character, on the other hand, rides the vicissitudes of life with even-mindedness. Personality endeavors to extract happiness from its experiences, whereas character realizes that happiness is an inherent quality of being that infuses experiences with happiness.

Your personality has been forged by the values of the external world beginning with parental fantasies about who you are and who you were raised to become, your education, your religions, your companions, all to assure your ego's survival and protection from getting hurt. Ego is an artifact that is used to fit in, to hang out in the status quo, an agreement with mediocrity that allows you to move and groove in the world without causing too much disturbance or being too much of an irritation. Eventually, such an existence becomes sterile, claustrophobic, painful. The way out is to learn how to ultimately tell the difference between your ego personality that is seeking to survive and avoid being hurt and your character that seeks to confidently deliver your talents, gifts, and skills. Remember, the ego seeks to protect the temporary personality by projecting unresolved issues such as a sense of separation from the whole, lack, and scarcity.

Do you sacrifice your individual spirit to comply with an agreement with mediocrity? The egoic consciousness of mediocrity rebels against excellence, saying, "Oh, that's not going to work. No other country in the world has succeeded in feeding all of its citizens!" "What, a 'green' house? Why, that wouldn't work with my seven flat screen TVs not to mention fertilizing my five acres of lawn!" Rebelling against new ideas, against new ways of being in the world is a complete lack of creativity that keeps our world enmeshed in false fear, useless wars, greed, and global warming.

Rather than surrender to the inner call of creativity, human nature tends to do the same things over and over again, even though centuries of existence have proven they don't work. "We're running out of–fill-in-the-blank–so let's create an excuse for invading a country that has what we need." It's *Ground Hog Day* all over again, doing what's already proven not to work for the individual or society.

## BECOMING A GENUINELY CIVILIZED SOCIETY

The good news is that more and more people are waking up and becoming creatively maladjusted. Not swimming in the shallow stream of society's values and diving instead into the deeper waters that many forerunners of social and spiritual liberation have introduced is the next expression of our becoming a genuinely civilized global society.

Arthur Schopenhauer, a nineteenth-century philosopher, made a powerful statement when he said that there all kinds of vices friends will forgive, such as a slovenly appearance, lateness, alcoholism, but they will not pardon our success. Sometimes personality won't let us go for greatness because it may result in alienation from those with whom we have close relationships; we may become disliked or resented for our changes by some of our intimates. Albert Einstein gave voice to this understanding when he said, "Arrows of hate have been shot at me, too; but they never hit me; because somehow they belong to another world, with which I have no connection whatsoever."[1]

Even if individuals become envious of us or resentful that we have grown beyond those things we once shared in common with them, such arrows cannot pierce us when we live in a higher vibrational frequency of being—when we have entered our true character. Living from our true character means that we draw an energetic circle large enough for everyone to fit into, even if we must love certain individuals at a distance.

### YOU: THE ONLY PERSON WITH WHOM YOU RELATE

As you take the time to observe yourself without judgment in various interactions and situations, you will be able to discern the motivation of your thoughts and subsequent actions. The more you become aware of the ways in which your personality has adapted to society, the more readily you can recalibrate your energetic responses so that they reflect your own unique soul-character. Then, whether it's in the workplace or at home, you will no longer say, "I have a relationship with my colleagues, my staff, my family, and my friends, and I deal with the problems they cause me all the time." No, you don't! You deal with only one individual: yourself. Your entire world of relating is with yourself.

This truth was literally "driven" home to me on an occasion when my wife, Rickie, and I were on our way to the airport. A woman pulled her car alongside our taxi and kept trying to get our driver's attention. We thought he just didn't notice and, because the other driver seemed to be in distress, we drew his attention to her. "Yeah, I see her," he grumbled. "She just wants me to let her get in front of us. So I'm ignoring her." Finally, at my persistence, he rolled down his window, whereupon she asked him for directions to a particular street. He wasn't dealing with her but rather with his own projections about her, which had only to do with himself.

What is the quality of your relationship with yourself? What is your relationship with creativity, peace, generosity, joy, excellence, spiritual practice? All of your so-called interactions with others are simply a reflection of your relationship with yourself and the soul-qualities that are seeking to express through you.

## THE PARADOX OF JOY

Are you satisfied that you are living at a level that expresses your soul-character? If not, then you are living out of integrity with your essential nature. You are not answering the deepest call of your being, which has nothing to do with outer circumstances such as what you own or whether or not people like you. Every time you actualize more of your potential by becoming more yourself, your joy increases, regardless of what's going on in your external circumstances. It's absolutely possible for your emotions to be running amok and to still be happy! It's possible for you to appear to be on a downward spiral, vacillating between sadness and disappointment, and yet to feel joy.

Circumstantially, you may be standing amidst the crash of breaking worlds while peace of mind simultaneously fills your awareness. Such a state of being requires that you drop complaining, bemoaning your fate, and blaming it on others. While you don't let people off the hook of accountability, you reclaim your power to participate in the unfolding of your destiny. It is your attitudes, formed by your beliefs, that are the filters through which you view your circumstances and even create them. As you begin to take full responsibility for your life, circumstances lose their power over you and you activate the dimension of your soul-character that yearns to express.

Step out of your thinking mind and begin to intuit what your Authentic Self yearns to express. This shift of awareness will out-picture as a new identity beyond the one that the world has assigned to you. This is how to liberate yourself from the accumulated identities under whose hypnotic spell you have been living. Realize that you are an individualized expression of the one life of Spirit that has become your very own Self. Then, what is happening cosmically begins to happen through you locally. That is when you will understand what the Buddha meant when he said that a human being is not a set of circumstances but a set of attitudes.

### WHAT'S RUNNING YOU?

It's easy to check in and find out if you're living in integrity with yourself. The question to ask yourself is, "What's running me?" It's quite revealing, even entertaining, to examine the personality programs and motivations that are unconsciously running you and causing you to conform to the world. Those reference points may be preventing you from entering a realm of intimacy and love, excellence, and vitality of character. The programs that operate in your life determine your experience. Be sure they're not blocking the excellence you want to live from. If you don't take some constructive action, your life will continue in its present mode and stall your growth and development. It's like rolling through your life with your brakes on. You may have a high vision for your life, but if your programming brakes are on, you won't budge.

A number of years ago I went for a bike ride with some members of my spiritual community. It was difficult for me to keep up with the group. Individuals kept riding to the end of the line and encouraging me. Peddling faster and harder just to stay even with everyone, I made a mental note to fortify my morning smoothie. Finally, we reached our destination, and when I got off my bike, I realized that I had been riding with my brakes on the entire time, preventing my effort from manifesting in a relaxed, enjoyable ride. In the same way, there are personality programs that are running us that are akin to riding through life with our mental-emotional brakes on. Is what's running you based on conscious or unconscious choices?

### STAND STRONG IN YOUR SOUL-CHARACTER

Begin to check yourself to see if you've allowed your personality to make so many adjustments that you no longer hear your unique soul-call. Perhaps you've become so fragmented that when you walk into a new situation the first thing you ask yourself—consciously or unconsciously—is, "How can I navigate myself through this situation so that I'm lookin' good?" In contrast, the creatively maladjusted aspirant asks, "How can I genuinely offer my heart in this environment?" This is how you begin to re-groove old programming and activate the evolutionary impulse within you to unfold your greater yet-to-be. Eventually, you will realize that the world didn't give you what is etched on your soul-character, nor can it take it away. Only you can choose to let it remain unexpressed.

When we study the lives of those individuals who had a strong, positive impact on society, we see that they somehow missed reading the book *How to Win Friends and Influence People*; they didn't always possess a pleasing personality by society's standards. What you will notice about such individuals is that they don't hang back waiting for approval from others in order to be themselves. Harriet Tubman, Bishop Desmond Tutu, Helen Keller, Rosa Parks, Susan B. Anthony, to name a few, are individuals who said "yes" to realizing the impossible dream, to reaching the unreachable star, and courageously expressing their purpose in life, their own unique soul-character.

### CHALLENGES ARE YOUR SPIRITUAL LIBERATORS

Many people believe that a challenge-free life is a happy life. However, life with its challenges stimulates our growth and development. Looking back over your life, you will have to admit that your growth was accelerated when you faced some form of suffering or pain that brought you to your wit's end. Such experiences hold the possibility of being catapulted from the small mind to the big mind.

Challenges reveal our blind spots, the places where we are yet bound by our personality traits and habitual thoughts of lack, limitation, and so on. The suffering caused by such mindsets motivates us to grow beyond them. If you think you don't have any problems, that there are no longer any inner valleys to forge, then although you may not have retired from life, you have retired from truly living. Being alive means welcoming the next challenge because you have discovered how this activates the evolutionary impulse to establish a higher vision for your life.

Transcending the personality's resistance to challenges is spiritually liberating. When you contemplate the challenges in your life, ask yourself, "*What gift within me is seeking to emerge?*" Place your attention on the emerging gift rather than the challenge and you will witness how the challenge begins to dissolve.

## ENTERING SPIRITUAL ADULTHOOD

As you mature spiritually, you ask life a different set of questions. Instead of, "Where can I find love?" you ask, "How can I radiate love?" You transcend wanting to be loved. It's natural to want to be loved, but when you mature, this desire doesn't develop into a needy personality. It shifts from desperately asking, "Isn't anybody going to ever love me?" to "How can I manifest and express more love in my life?" *Then, from the center of your Self there will radiate a divine love so potent that you will begin to fall in love with being loving and no longer limit yourself to having to have an object to love.* You discover that life itself is infiltrated with love, that love exists in every dimension of your existence because you no longer depend on love showing up in an external way. You love for the sake of loving. You transcend the personality's definitions and the needs that have been ruling your world. You gain dominion over your existence where love is concerned.

## HUMAN AND TRANSCENDENT

A human incarnation is precious, magnificent. Do not dismiss the human experience for the transcendent experience—both are our destiny. Become a conscious artist of your life through the medium of your human incarnation. Your incarnation is your canvas. Own it! As you continue to awaken, you will become creatively maladjusted. You will no longer fit into your world of yesterday. And just when you think you've arrived at a particular level of growth, you will understand that there's more of your Self to be realized and expressed, that while you have come so far and evolved through many challenges, you've barely scratched the surface of your ultimate magnificence. The filters through which you receive and interpret life obliterate, and you contact each moment just as it is. You no longer superimpose your thoughts about reality onto Reality.

An interviewer once asked me, "What is it we must do when we get snared into reacting from our personality traits?" My response was simple: "Ask yourself some questions: What is it that I am to discern in this situation? What opportunity is here that I'm not grasping? What good is here that I am not seeing?" Your life unfolds, in part, according to the type of questions you place before yourself. By asking relevant questions, you will then activate the eye behind the eye, the ear behind the ear, the mind behind the mind. A whole new world of insight, beauty, intelligence, and intuition will spring into expression through you.

## ARE YOU A THERMOMETER OR A THERMOSTAT?

You will also come to understand what Dr. Martin Luther King Jr. meant when he described some people as being thermometers and others as thermostats, which is to say that there are those who give a reading as to what's going on, while others set the temperature. You are here to set the temperature, to impute the vibration that changes the atmosphere you inhabit. Raise the volume and live out loud in such a way that your character informs your expressions in this world. Take your cues from the internal guidance of your spirit, not from the external values of a world gone mad. You will not only take a reading of what's going on in society, you will reset the temperature to one that honors the dignity of all beings, that contributes to world citizenry.

Perhaps, up to this moment, you have adjusted very successfully to society's dictates and are concerned that you might get carried away or lose yourself if you enter a new way of being. Put your mind at rest. Being creatively maladjusted does not mean that you become an outlaw, a total rebel against society. No. It means you don't fit into society so well that you're not of any evolutionary good, that you make no imprint on the planet that advances its "progress."

Creatively maladjusted individuals become distribution centers of the highest potential that is seeking to emerge during their time in human history. Your life's successes may not be recorded in the pages of history. Your name may not be emblazoned on a marble wall. But the vibrational imprint of your elegance of character will be a legacy in every corner of the cosmos. Break free from the artifacts of ego. What does it matter if your heart is so generous that people think you're off your rocker? Some may tell you not to give to a homeless person, that you work too hard for your money to give it away, that the hours you are serving as a Big Brother or a Big Sister mentor could be spent improving your golf swing. Mediocrity at its highest!

To live in a consciousness that sees with the inner eye and hears with the inner ear cannot be taught. It can only be caught on the radar of your inner spiritual practices, in the silent recesses of your soul. Give yourself permission to stop long enough to enter the inner sky of your being and commune with the Self in meditation, affirmative prayer, visioning, and contemplation. Through selfless service learn how to expand your heart. This is how you will become a spiritual thermostat and consciously set the temperature of what is happening in your life no matter what the thermometer of the outside world reads.

## STEP OUT OF THE THINKING MIND

Perhaps you already have a rich inner practice. What I've learned through my own practice is, regardless of how far I have come, all the obstacles I've transcended, I've barely scratched the surface. I don't say this to discourage you or to discount my experience or anyone's progress, but because we are on an *eternal* adventure, even when we realize that we are pure awareness, there is work left to be done.

Step out of your thinking mind and begin to contemplate what your true character yearns to express. This shift of awareness will outpicture as a new identity beyond the one that the world has assigned you. Liberate yourself from the accumulated identities under whose hypnotic spell you have been living. You are an individualized expression of Spirit that has become your very own Self.

As you continue to deepen your inner work through your spiritual practices, study, fellowship, and service, you will increasingly become creatively maladjusted. You will be counted among those who have not sold out their spirit to a world that knows not how to handle such a precious commodity.

Are you willing to activate the creatively maladjusted within you? If so, prepare to release the baggage you're carrying from societal conditioning. Take the brakes off, throw away the rearview mirror that only sees the past, and live the life you were destined for. You are here to become free and live a life of excellence at all levels. And the world will be better for this because one man, one woman, said "yes" to their soul-character and dared to reach for the unreachable star, to live in the impossible dream.

### Affirmation

*Today, I confidently step out of my comfort zone. I let go of self-consciousness and egoic concerns as I express myself freely, fully. I dedicate myself to genuine self-expression and know the joy of being my true self.*

## Embodiment

In this moment, I begin again. Each and every day I awaken to a new beginning, to a new aspect of myself where creativity is concerned, where discovering my authentic being is concerned. I am set free today—free to come out of the box of my habitual way of relating to myself, to others, and to life itself.

My consciousness now reflects back to me the truth that I am not my circumstances. I am not my emotions. I am not the thoughts that are moving through me. I hear that part of me that knows its infinite nature speaking now, encouraging me to court that which is seeking to emerge through me, that which is yearning to express my individuality, my own unique creative nature. It is the mark of the Spirit etched in my soul-character. I set it free now. It's okay for it to emerge. It's okay for me to become more of who I am.

With this permission I have given myself, I know that my life is attuned to the fundamental order of existence. My entire being is now reshaping itself around this "yes" factor of my willingness to be whole, beautiful, and authentic. Every cell, every organ, every action, and every function of my being is receiving and embodying this message. Any conscious and unconscious fears or doubts are even now being transmuted into courage and enthusiasm. Outlets for my creative nature seek me out and I willingly respond to them. New ideas flow through me, insights unfold within me. It's happening right now.

I understand what it means to be creatively maladjusted, and there is no hesitancy within me to express my uniqueness as an individualized expression of the Spirit. In this feeling tone, the strongholds of self-consciousness are dissolving. Liberation is the order of my day. My consciousness absorbs the power of this word. My energetic being is wrapping itself around this frequency.

No longer do I look to newspapers, trends, or outside sources to tell me who and what I ought to be, how I ought to look, what I should buy. From this moment forward, I look within and realize that my own Self is the leaping-off point for my creativeness. I go homeward within and acquaint myself with dimensions of my being I have never before encountered. I lovingly welcome them to outpicture in my life, to express fully and freely.

I set my own inner thermostat to a temperature in which I thrive, in which the love that I am flourishes. The joy that I am saturates all that I think, say, and do. I am a conscious co-creator of my destiny. My thoughts are no longer determined by the thoughts of others. My inner sense of empowerment is no longer dependent upon the praise of others. I break the chains that bind me to any sense of mediocrity, to any sense of follower-ship where I give my power away mentally, emotionally, socially, religiously, physically. I am pulled by the Spirit's vision for my life. I hear it; I respond to it. I incorporate its intuitive guidance in my life. Everything now works together for my good. I am comfortable, at ease in this inner freedom. My consciousness is causative, unfolding my character, my destiny, in a most magnificent way.

How precious it is to know that I am divinely, unconditionally supported by the universe, that this Existence mothers me, that all of my needs are met. In the midst of me is divine love, compassion, wisdom, peace, and joy. My Source is internal, not external.

Control and manipulation are no longer necessary to get my needs met because I now recognize that all that I need to free myself has already been given. With a heart filled with gratitude, I simply say, "Thank you, Infinite Spirit."

## Note

1. Albert Einstein, *Out of My Later Years* (New York: Philosophical Library, 1950).

# 9
# Architects of the Beloved Community

*I live to be the message that I long to see*
*I long to be the way that I'm looking for*
*I need to shine the light that I want to see*

I enjoy researching the dictionary definition of words because I frequently find in their etymologies spiritual overtones that increase my appreciation for how the vibrational power of language motivates individuals and entire communities to take life-transforming action. A perfect example was when I was contemplating my talk for "Season for Nonviolence," an annual program that celebrates the work and life of Dr. Martin Luther King Jr. and Mohandas K. Gandhi. In my research, I learned that the word *community* comes from the Latin *communitas*. *Communitas* is derived from *communis*, a combination of the Latin prefix *com*, which means "together," and *munis*, which involves the performance of services.

The term "Beloved Community" was coined in the early twentieth century by the philosopher-theologian Josiah Royce, founder of the Fellowship of Reconciliation, an organization that remains active today as one of the largest interfaith groups in the United States dedicated to the promotion of peace and nonviolence.

Dr. Martin Luther King Jr., a member of the Reconciliation, gave Beloved Community a more profound meaning by associating it with agape love, and in a 1959 sermon, he formally declared a core value of his community to be Agape love: "This type of love can transform opponents into friends. It is this love which will bring about miracles in the hearts of men."

**IT'S HAPPENING NOW!**

During my travels speaking and teaching over the last few years, I have witnessed a global shift in consciousness. It reverberated in my conversations with the citizens of South Africa, Ghana, Brazil, Cuba, Peru, and Sri Lanka. In India and Italy, I was privileged to facilitate and serve on panels with His Holiness the Dalai Lama, scientists, economists, futurists, and spiritual leaders from many traditions. We each contributed insights to determine what it would take—individually and collectively—to address our urgent global challenges, to create a world where the dignity and uniqueness of all peoples would be recognized and honored, to preserve the Earth's resources and stop the extinction of the species.

In 2007, I accepted an invitation to participate in the one-million-person Peace Meditation organized by Dr. A. T. Ariyaratne, founder of the Sarvodaya Shramadana Movement in Sri Lanka. (In Sanskrit, *sarvodaya* means "everybody wakes up.") His purpose was to bring peace to the factions fighting within his country. The results were tangible and immediate: both sides agreed to go to Geneva for peace talks.

In 2007, I also participated in The Peace Alliance in Washington, D.C., a grassroots movement in which my friend and colleague Marianne Williamson was heavily involved in placing a bill before the U.S. House of Representatives to establish a Department of Peace. At the time of this writing, twenty cities representing 7.4 million Americans have joined The Peace Alliance. Imagine in the foreseeable future having a Secretary of Peace to advise the president during times of crisis, offering him or her options other than violent solutions to national and international conflict.

A national survey, the Zogby Poll, sponsored in 2007 by the National Council of Crime and Delinquency, a leading criminal justice research organization, revealed that by nearly an eight to one margin, the U.S. voting public favors rehabilitation services for prisoners during incarceration and upon release rather than punishment.

What, except an acceleration in the evolution of the global collective consciousness, can explain why, everyday people are voluntarily enlisting as spiritual revolutionaries, participating in what Dr. Martin Luther King Jr. called a "revolution of values"? One common denominator is rallying humanity to implement initiatives toward peace; to resolve clashes among cultures, races, religious paths, and governments, and to preserve the planet's resources and species: *the growing realization that our continued survival depends upon dispelling the illusion that we are separate from one another, that the borders between countries are real.*

## LOVE: THE ULTIMATE CONQUEROR

As the realization that we are members of a world family finds its home in more and more hearts, people across the globe are dissolving manmade boundaries and acknowledging our interconnectedness. They are announcing that now is the time to bring a halt to dehumanizing Earth's inhabitants, that now is the time to put an end to world hunger, wars, inadequate healthcare, lack of education, global warming. Architects of the Beloved Community are spiritual revolutionaries who realize that the solution to global challenges is a spiritual one, that conquest through war is at best temporary; only conquest by love is permanent.

Love is not an emotion, a romantic notion; it is a living, organically powerful energy that holds together the fabric of the created world. Love is what we are. The world is looking for love masters, and each of us is that potential love master. Egocentric points of view must give way to world-centric points of view, to a more expanded mind-set beyond "me and mine." As Thomas R. Kelly put it, "The relation of each to all, in God, is real, objective, existential. It is our eternal relationship that is shared by every stick and stone and bird and beast and saint and sinner in the universe."

Awakening our inherent love-nature can be messy and uncomfortable. We are often unaware of when and how low-level anxiety overtakes our minds. We've accepted that it's normal to be tense, upset, reactionary, fearful, doubt-filled, and worried. We don't want to deny what is going on around us—that people are starving; that AIDS is ravaging the lives of men, women, and children in parts of the world; that wars are taking place; that terrorism exists; that slavery still exists; that there are people who cause harm. What is required to begin shifting these external facts is maintaining a focus on individual inner change. Through our individual inner work, we discover that we have ample gifts to contribute to establishing an enlightened society. We then become motivated to deliver these gifts in a mind-set of love, not out of fear that the world needs saving. *We are not here to "save" the world, but to serve an emerging paradigm of love, connectedness, and generosity of heart.* The egoic structure feeds on fear and separation, archaic notions that sweep across our individual and global landscapes. Fear escalates negative change while love escalates affirmative change. Love is the antidote to fear-based approaches.

## COUNTERCULTURAL VALUES ARE STILL ALIVE

Before you think my head is buried in the sand of denial, I am well aware of what is going on in the world. We can't avoid the media's message of doom and gloom on radio and television news, in newspapers and magazines. At the time of this writing, the United States is at war with Iraq with thousands of men, women, and children from both sides uselessly dying, causing unbearable sorrow to their loved ones. We are all aware of what is happening in Israel and Gaza, Tibet and China, Burma, Pakistan, India, the challenges that exist throughout Africa and in the United States.

While all this is sadly true, it is also one-sided in the sense that we don't commonly hear about movements and individuals who are putting their lives on the line for peace, individuals who use technology as a communication tool for raising the collective consciousness, for ending world hunger. We don't hear about how millions of individuals are shifting their views from war and other world tragedies and towards ecological building materials and preserving the Earth's resources. Instead, we hear about societal fashions and other superficiality created by the media as they compete with tabloid news. The corporate media is not a vehicle for appreciative inquiry. It's no wonder that so many individuals depend upon alternative sources for their news.

In the '60s, "counterculture" was the term used for a person who was considered unpatriotic, radical, a troublemaker. This terminology may still disturb some people because it indicates going counter to the culture in which one lives. When one's country is wronged—or one's family, for that matter—the cultural values of patriotism and loyalty translate into taking names, kicking butt, protecting, suing, making certain somebody pays for the injustices committed. Countercultural values turn these approaches upside down with love, compassion, forgiveness, mediation, reconciliation. Spiritual revolutionaries see the inefficacy of the old approaches.

The technological revolution has contributed to the awareness that we live in a global village. Our world can change and reshape itself like at no other time in history. In fact, it is already doing so. However, technology in the hands of those who apply its advances to create sophisticated warheads is misused. Such "peace-keeping" weapons will not bring peace. "Ultimate peace will come," said Paramahansa Yogananda, "when, by mutual agreement, all nations of the Earth will have continued peace conferences, and will scrap their weapons and instead help to destroy the Earth's slums."[1]

This doesn't mean that individuals or countries should not be held accountable for their wrongdoing, but why not conduct negotiations and make reparations before retaliatory, punitive actions are taken that contribute to the cycle of further suffering, to devaluing the sacredness of human existence? Why make war the first line of defense?

I am not advocating pacifism at any cost or cowardice. I join the ranks of those who agree with one of the world's most radical revolutionaries, Jesus the Christ, who encourages us to love our seeming enemies, to bless those who curse us, who hate us, and to pray for those who persecute us. We can follow the example of the Dalai Lama who prays for the Chinese government even as they oppress the Tibetan people and force him and other Tibetans to live in exile.

Nuclear warheads are being developed throughout the world because world leaders live by the Darwinian theory of survival of the fittest. War is justified under the guise of protecting national borders, resources, jobs, customs, and religious beliefs. The upheavals, wars, and rumors of wars being played out in various parts of the world are fear-based, power-hungry reactions founded on a lack of understanding of the truth that we are all one.

Yet, in the midst of it all, something is seeking to emerge. To paraphrase Emanuel Swedenborg, God suffers from a stillbirth until we act by the good he already knows. The "good" we already know thunders through the voices and examples of spiritual revolutionaries whose truths rise above the discordant screams of war, hatred, fear, and ignorance. Love dissolves borders of all kinds—physical, mental, and spiritual.

## LIFE IN THE "ZERO" LANE

Mohandas K. Gandhi entered the ranks of a spiritual revolutionary when he was thrown off a train in South Africa. An educated lawyer with all the outer trappings he thought earned him a first-class seat, suddenly he found himself lying in the dirt, his belongings strewn all around him and people yelling, "How dare you, a lowly Indian, try to ride in a first-class coach!" Later in his life he said, "Only when you become a 'zero' can you know fearlessness." Becoming a zero is radical behavior because you come into contact with something larger than you ever recognized yourself as being and capable of doing. More and more individuals are gravitating toward applying the same power of good that inspired this scrawny but determined vegetarian known as Gandhi to transform an entire nation and free it from the shackles of colonialism.

More and more individuals are waking up and adding their voices to those of earlier spiritual warriors who teach forgiveness, peace, compassion, love, and reconciliation, proving that spiritual principle thrives in spite of every opposition to it.

Through our freedom of choice, we have been given the capacity to create and to destroy. If destruction, which is based on fear and ignorance, were more powerful than spiritual wisdom, our planet would have been destroyed aeons ago. Humanity's continued existence bears witness to the power of Good, which is the power of God, the Love-Intelligence governing the cosmos.

### ORDINARY PEOPLE CAN RESPOND IN AN EXTRAORDINARY WAY

Let us not make excuses for ourselves. Dr. Ariyaratne, Gandhi, Dr. King, the Dalai Lama, and other emissaries of peace, such as Nelson Mandela, Rigoberta Menchú, Dolores Huerta, Bishop Desmond Tutu, Cesar Chavez, and Thich Nhat Hanh, are all ordinary people who have responded to life in an extraordinary way. Their mothers weren't virgins; they didn't arrive on the planet by special means. They're human beings like you and me. It is not necessary to don monastic robes or clerical collars or to wear garlands around your neck to be counted among the growing number of spiritual revolutionaries. Those who practice peace principles are accountants, janitors, artists, plumbers, professors, poets, and nurses. Being a spiritualrevolutionary has gone mainstream and expresses through simple acts of kindness, patience, and generosity of heart.

Your life is as significant as the greatest harbingers of peace. You are as cherished by the Spirit as any avatar, master, or saint who ever walked the planet. When you think and act from a spiritualized consciousness, you are have joined the revolution of values and serve as a beneficial presence on the planet. When revolutionary values kick in, you prioritize your time differently, you allocate your financial resources differently, you use your talents differently. No longer are you simply furthering the goals of the little self; you recognize the One Life that walks through all feet and so include the good of all in your own. Your life takes on a depth of purpose. The energy you invest in this transformation will yield rich returns.

The Self of each individual already contains all that is required for individual and planetary peace. Spiritual revolutionaries have awakened to this truth; they rebel against the hypocrisy in humankind's economic, social, governmental, educational, familial, and religious life structures.

### BEGIN RIGHT WHERE YOU ARE

Architects of the Beloved Community release a vibration of love wherever they go—in the line at the market, on the freeway, at the gym, in the workplace, in the presence of so-called enemies. They reveal the highest love-potential of the human spirit. With increasing commitment, let us wrap our awareness around the preciousness of human life and devote our energies to realizing our oneness with our brothers and sisters on the planet.

One of the most tender experiences you will encounter on the path of a spiritual revolutionary is the realization that you are never walking alone. You are walking with the Infinite, the Power, and the Presence within all that exists. This awareness enables you to move through society as a transforming agent who dares to stand in spiritual integrity announcing the truth that love is the law of life. That is why, long after they leave this three-dimensional world, we remain in reverential awe of great lovers of humankind who instigated a revolution of values that changed the vibration of the time in which they lived. They teach us that there is no separation between our political endeavor, social endeavor, and spiritual endeavor. All is to be governed by the immutable principle that we are indeed one global family co-creating the destiny of our planet. Then watch your spark of practice become a wildfire of awakening, a torrent of divine love and compassion that uplifts the world.

Every time we express love, everytime we give up resentments and animosity, every time we forgive, every time we serve others, every time we share our resources, every time we put others first, we walk the path of the spiritual revolutionary. We don't have to "get our act together" to become a beneficial presence on the planet. We come just as we are. Take your stand as a spiritual revolutionary and participate in the revolution of values as you cultivate a heart of love as wide as the world.

## SKILLFUL MEANS FOR BUILDING THE BELOVED COMMUNITY

The first skillful means we need to develop is awareness. By cultivating awareness, you begin to see how and where you habitually invest your energy. The ego tries to convince us that it's about "them, them, them," a blaming mentality. Then it escalates to "I'll show them," which becomes an adversarial position. For a few seconds, this feels good. However, as you become aware that you are operating from fear, you will notice that such an aggressive attitude causes your whole being to contract. You tense up and cut yourself off from spontaneity, creativity, clear thinking.

The second skillful means is to free yourself from the common worldview and discover your own viewpoints independent of popular opinion. Don't wait for the politicians, pundits, spiritual teachers, and motivational speakers to give you permission. It rests with each of us to begin right within ourselves. The Beloved Community is even now alive within our collective heart and soul. When we broadcast love out into our world, then as surely as the day follows the night, we will see that the Beloved Community breaks out wherever we go.

## BE THE CHANGE YOU WANT TO SEE

Become an emissary of love, peace, kindness, and generosity. To paraphrase Dr. King, the Beloved Community does not roll in on wheels of inevitability. It rolls on the backs of those who are willing to become the change they want to see, those who are willing to co-create with Existence the change they desire. As each one of us grows up and takes self-responsibility for evolving our individual consciousness, life will become viewed as sacred. We will practice Here-and-Now-ism knowing that in this very moment we are interpenetrated by a loving Presence looking back at itself through our eyes.

The Beloved Community is based on the awareness that we are One, that we are the world, not simply when we hold hands and sing the song, but when we live by the universal spiritual principle of oneness. Set your aspiration to actively become a contributing architect of the Beloved Community.

### AFFIRMATION

*I know that my true essence is love, divine love. Such a potency of love am I that, were I to realize its fullness, I would be on my knees before my own inner self. Today, I embrace all of my brothers and sisters in this love. I wrap myself and every man, woman, and child in this love. I have no enemies, imagined or real. I practice world citizenry and radiate out a blessing of love upon the planet.*

### EMBODIMENT

Right here and right now, I call forth a revolution in my consciousness. I experience a revolution in my mind that now realizes its oneness with all beings, all life. My soul pours out a blessing to all my brothers and sisters on the planet. In consciousness, I wrap my spiritual arms around everyone, those who call themselves my family, my friends, even my enemies. I expand this awareness to include my entire neighborhood, my community, my city, my state, my country, and my world.

I acknowledge myself as a member of the Beloved Community that includes the entire globe. All beings are my brothers and sisters; all creatures are my relatives. This truth of my oneness with all life is awakened in my consciousness as never before. The spiritual astigmatism is removed from my inner sight, and I not only sense and know my oneness with all beings, I respond to it. Everything shines brighter through the lens of this realization, leading me to make new choices, to take new actions. I freely share of my heart, time, energy, and resources with my world.

No longer do I give my power to society's opinions. I release my false identity and now know myself to be what Existence means for me to be: a self-responsible, self-realized being. That which is real about me—love, compassion, peace, generosity—asserts itself uniquely in, through, and as me. This is not simply a mental exercise. It takes the form of action that emanates from my heart. I begin today in simple ways to express love and generosity of spirit. I now see opportunities all around me to give of myself, to serve my brothers and sisters.

I am fed and nourished by a vision of peace on the planet, beginning within my own heart. When I am tempted to choose impatience, I choose patience. When I am tempted to choose retaliation, I choose reconciliation. When I see in the news images of those who are suffering and in sorrow, I send out a blessing to heal their hearts. I send out a blessing to the leaders of countries who imagine themselves to be dictators of their people, holding them in bondage. I declare that their misunderstanding of genuine power shifts right now. Where countries fight over boundaries, I see false divisions dissolving. Battles over historical or religious rights are set aside, and cooperation and harmony are now the order of the day.

And it is in this awareness that I realize the preciousness of human life. I send out a blessing to all of my brothers and sisters on the planet. May they know peace, inner fulfillment. May they all have food, water, clothing, and education. Above all, may they know love, may they realize their own inner self and express their unique gifts and talents. My prayer is that all beings may be free, free to fully participate in the joy of existence.

I fearlessly walk through life, daring to go against the crowd. I count myself in the number of spiritual revolutionaries. I don't just meditate upon peace, love, and oneness; I practice it in my daily life. I am in service to a spiritual idea called peace, spiritual ideas called forgiveness, compassion, lovingkindness. I bless the world's leaders that they catch a spiritual idea of peace, harmony, and wholeness, that they yield to it and realize that heaven can be experienced on earth. I see in my mind's eye a world that prepares not for war but for celebration of all the blessings contained in the preciousness of a human incarnation.

Today, love flows through me uninterruptedly, spontaneously, freely. I go with this current of love and allow it to flood away any fear, insecurity, animosity, jealousy, resentment. Love, peace, harmony, understanding, patience—these byproducts of love are today my teachers, and I am their worthy student and servant. And so it is, and so I let it be.

## NOTE

1. Paramahansa Yogananda, *The Divine Romance* (Los Angeles: Self-Realization Fellowship, 1986).

# 10
# Don't Get Serious, Get Real

*I thank you for being so real and changing me*
*Opening my time-blinded eyes to see*
*My glorious possibilities*

Has anyone ever told you that you take yourself too seriously? Or maybe you remember a past conversation when you confided to a friend, "Oh, he takes himself so seriously that it's hard to be around him." Serious people believe everything that they think and feel, even without examining what underlies their thoughts, feelings, or beliefs. Not questioning one's answers about life can seem like a safe and secure way to live, but such an approach will not place you in touch with Reality.

Think of a time when you felt very serious. Wasn't it accompanied by a sense of being constricted, tight, shut down? Then compare it to a time when you were feeling joyous. Didn't you feel free and expansive? Individuals who take themselves very seriously bring up, for me, a visual of Auguste Rodin's *The Thinker*, the monumental sculpture he created for a group work titled *The Gates of Hell*. There he sits all bent over, tensed up, chin in hand, heavily thinking with an expression that looks like Excedrin headache number forty-seven is pounding in his head. The work is so convincing you can almost hear him saying, "I'm a thinker, and I'm thinking my way into solving the mystery of existence."

In contrast, it always brings a smile to my mind when I substitute that image with that of Siddhartha Gautama, who became a Buddha, meaning "awakened one." There he sits, buoyantly floating on a lotus flower, a blissful smile on his face because he woke up to the Real—no quandaries, no seriousness. He reduced his awareness to the utter simplicity of Being. The weight of judgments, opinions, beliefs, and concepts were replaced by pure awareness of the Real. (Just writing this practically transports me into a joyous state of consciousness!)

## THE NECTAR OF LAUGHTER

Speaking of the Buddha, I'm reminded of a story I heard about a Zen teacher who studied the dharma and meditated for many, many years. His students said that when he became enlightened he laughed for two solid days, developing such a spasm he nearly died from laughter. Laughter takes us out of time. For a microsecond, we become extemporal, transported into the gap, a timeless dimension of the Real where we aren't caught, snagged, or snared by our narrow little perceptions, points of view, cherished beliefs, thinking our way into rationalizing, and justifying our existence.

Laughter is nectar that flows directly from the soul. It has nothing to do with our circumstances. When we laugh, we touch our inner luminosity. Laughter liberates us from the thinking mind and presents us with precious moments of spontaneous meditation where there arises a super-aliveness. Laughter transports us back to an inherent memory of oneness with all life, before all of our conditioning into "normalcy" began. When our laughter is absolutely genuine, we can hear the whisper of our inner spirit assuring us that we may recapture our joy, that we may reclaim our original nature made in the image and likeness of Spirit and be a conscious co-creator, an artist of our own life.

Meanwhile, it is very healthy to be able to laugh at ourselves. If you have difficulty doing this, then ask a few of your friends what they laugh at about you behind your back. They aren't being two-faced, because more often than not, these qualities endear you to them. If they're really honest, they'll tell you and give you a great opportunity to laugh at yourself.

Recently, Rickie, my wife, was playfully making fun of how I speak, claiming that I'm a media person's nightmare. Then she began imitating my antics, like how I move around on the dais when speaking. "You run over here, you jump in the air, you dance. They're even threatening to draw a circle on the dais floor to keep you within its parameters!" Someone who really loves you will help you to good-naturedly laugh at yourself and shake off, loosen up your all-caught-upness about your self-image. They also shine a light on those aspects of ourselves that we haven't quite refined, where our potential has not yet fully actualized. Humor is the beginning of wisdom, and wisdom introduces us to Reality.

## REALITY WITH A CAPITAL "R"

Becoming awakened is the realization of the real, not the realistic or real-like, but real with a capital "R." The Real is the eternal, intangible, inconceivable, unimaginable wholeness that has been buried under the weight of our ignorance about who and what we really are.

Sadly, in the West, individuals have been raised under a false concept of having been born in original sin, which is one of the greatest perpetrations upon humanity. There is no such thing as original "sin." What is called sin is actually original ignorance, acting from a state of ignorance of our true nature, which means a false belief in a sense of separation from our Source. We are not intrinsically flawed! How can this be so when we are fully franchised expressions of Infinite Beauty, made in the image and likeness of the Spirit, of its Wholeness?

In the East, individuals are burdened with a belief in bad karma. The law of karma works in such a way that what we put out into the world returns to us. In contemporary parlance, what goes around comes around. Karma does not determine our destiny. Our karma can only determine a starting point, but it can never determine our destiny. Our destiny is determined by our attitude and character, which are constantly being formed through our moment-by-moment choices. Our attitudes form our character, and our character determines our destiny. So regardless of the mistakes we have made, we do not have to languish in a belief system that states, "I'm suffering in this lifetime because of errors from previous incarnations." No! As you evolve, your destiny changes because destiny is a dynamic, energetic flux.

## FROM CONCRETIZING TO SPIRITUAL DISCERNMENT

In my own inner spiritual walk, I have discovered that, as human beings, we move through four stages of perceiving reality. The first and most basic is the beginning level of what I call concretizing the infinite. For example, if I say the word "God," an image of a man sitting on a throne with a long, gray beard may form in your mind. If you're not quite that visual, there is nevertheless a sense of a presence sitting in judgment of you, watching your every move, reading your every thought, metaphorically shaking an invisible finger in your face. Therein lies the source of the pain of guilt, shame, anxiety, the embarrassment of being who you are, giving birth to the "If they really knew me they would..." syndrome. And it is not entirely our fault. We have been taught to think in these limited, shame-producing ways since we were children. This is the work of religion, not spirituality. *Religion is comprised of concrete dogmas, while spirituality is comprised of direct realization of the Real.*

We also tend to concretize our concept of supply—our material resources—and relate to it in terms of money. Because we think that we know what we want, we visualize the material things we imagine will make us comfortable and content. We make dream boards, speak our affirmations, and participate in superficial magical thinking without any priority given to the longing of our inner spirit to wake up. We have little interest in the gifts of divinity that long to be stirred into expression through us. Simultaneously, we're confused about why we're *still* not happy once our material desires are fulfilled. We don't yet realize that there is never enough of that which doesn't satisfy. We think the answer is to accumulate yet more. When achieving this "more" still doesn't satisfy, we begin to catch that there must be a deeper place to go within ourselves for authentic peace of mind.

## APPROACHING THE ABSTRACT

The next level of consciousness we move into is a more abstract conceptualization of the Infinite. We begin to contemplate the qualities of the Spirit as being more abstract, such as love, peace, harmony, compassion, wisdom. We engage the personal mind and intellect. Intellect doesn't solve anything; it just keeps rearranging the deck chairs on the Titanic. Intelligence is not the result of the intellect, which is an aspect of the mind. Intelligence is a soul-faculty of consciousness. While theologians may intellectually touch upon the abstract, mystics commune with the Real, merging their consciousness with its qualities. Theologians may argue, but mystics agree.

In the mystical awareness, one hears the inaudible and sees the invisible, not with the senses but with the soul-faculties. Then there is no need to argue; there is nothing left to argue about because the soul knows, and knows that it knows, what it has realized in deep communion with the Self.

Many mystics use the word *beloved* when attempting to share their realization of ecstatic communion. Their poetry and writings use anthropomorphic language in an attempt to describe the indescribable because it is the closest they can come to expressing the intimate nature of the Impersonal. Even reading the works of Rumi, Kabir, Hafiz, Mirabai, St. Theresa of Avila, and St. John the Divine can transport us to a blissful state.

### ARTISTIC PERCEPTIVITY: THE REALM OF LUMINOSITY

Eventually, we tire of mere intellectualizing and move into the third realm of artistic perceptivity. Artistic perceptivity provides individuals the capacity to "see" beauty, the energy of luminous perfection behind a seemingly imperfect world. It enables us to see the indescribable. As a soulful artist, our inner vision begins to penetrate the world of concrete appearances. We perceive the fluidity of the cosmos and that of our own consciousness. We become prone to making works of art out of the simplest and complex everyday activities.

Take, for example, the difference between a composer and a musician. The musician interprets a song, and that is beautiful. The composer has attuned himself to a sound that is inaudible, that is caught by the soul-faculty of intuitive listening and translated into music. This is how Beethoven, who began going deaf at around twenty-eight years of age, continued to compose music. The great Sufi master and musician Hazrat Inayat Khan went so far as to write in his book *The Mysticism of Sound and Music*, "Composition is an art rather than a mechanical arrangement of notes. The work of the composer of music is no less than the work of a saint. The composer needs tenderness of heart, open eyes to all beauty, the true perception of sound and rhythm and its expression in human nature."[1]

You are here to activate that same soul-perception within yourself, to compose your own music as you inwardly attune yourself to the beat and rhythm of your individuality, and to prepare to enter the fourth stage of spiritual discernment.

## SPIRITUAL DISCERNMENT

Spiritual discernment is a direct, intuitive perception of the Real. Seers, sages, beholders, and mystics occupy this realm. Jesus the Christ, to our knowledge, did not paint; he did not write a sermon. His life was his artwork, a portrait of all that is divine within us. And like the other illumined beings, he set an example of a non-dual way of moving in the world. He had an artist's perceptivity and a mystical awareness with sight beyond the two eyes, hearing beyond the two ears, touch beyond the hands. "Most assuredly, I say unto you, he who believes in me, the works that I do he will do also: and greater works than these he will do," he said in all humility.[2] He left us with a clear statement that we too are fully equipped to live life from the dimension of Reality. When we cultivate spiritual discernment, we yield fully to the Divine Artist and make our life a great work of art.

## FROM EYESIGHT TO INSIGHT

Through meditation we transcend the personal mind and begin to see not with eyesight but with insight. It is similar to the way Beethoven heard perfectly orchestrated symphonies with his inner ear of intuition. Symphonies surround us; they sing to us of our inner beauty, our potential, our utmost fulfillment.

When you realize that the Spirit individualized itself and named itself you, you unhook yourself from nonsense, such as what others are thinking about you, even what you are thinking about yourself. Instead, you begin to ask, "How is the Spirit of Life functioning in, through, and as me?" Place that question before the tribunal of your consciousness more and more frequently, and you will begin to attune yourself to insights from the realm of the Real. You will break the thought-chain of belief in a personal mind, a mind filled with self-doubts that hold you hostage and cause lack of fulfillment. It is possible to end that false cycle of thinking *right now* if you are willing to deepen, to make your spiritual practices a priority.

### EMERGENCE WITHOUT EMERGENCY

Suffering is a great awakener. Human beings go through excruciating circumstances. Even so, you will often hear individuals describe how their lives were changed for the better because of them. Odd as it may sound, suffering has its own gifts that are different but equally as valuable as the gifts that happiness gives us. However, we can emerge from ignorance to wisdom, from pain to joy, from sickness to health, without waiting for a personal emergency to motivate us. Love, joy, peace, compassion, wisdom—these inherent qualities can be stirred within us in an instant of receptivity to the Real. Then, we become conscious artists of life in a co-creative partnership with the Real, discerning Reality and acting from that dimension.

### RADICAL ALIVENESS

Many people live by the mantra, "I have drama; therefore, I am alive." If their calendars are filled to overflowing and their cell phones are ceaselessly ringing, they are convinced that they are living life to the fullest, when in actuality they are skimming the surface of existence. Business, unending socializing, and entertainment has become confused with aliveness. Speediness, doingness, over-stimulation is not aliveness.

Radical aliveness begins when we wake up to the realization that there is no personal power, there is no personal good, and there is no private good. There is no personal power because there is only the One Power operating through us and enlivening all creation. It is this Power that, when properly understood, empowers us from within to express who and what we really are. If we are honest with ourselves, we will admit that we have a misunderstanding about power which in turn leads us to wield personal power over others and to engage in power struggles with them.

How many times have you thought you wanted to be better than someone else, to outsmart someone else? How often do you fantasize about being a mover and shaker in the worldly sense? This is all a virus that infects us because of our misunderstanding about power as it is defined by a society that thrives on consumerism and materialism, a society in which it is easy to become snagged in endless desire for superiority to dispel a sense of inferiority. But there is no superiority to be had. We don't, however, have to condemn ourselves for succumbing to thought-forms of wanting to be "better than." All we have to do is realize that those thoughts are broadcast from the ego and not take ownership of them.

Forgive yourself by realizing that the illusion of false power is thick and sticky, and you just got a little on you. So what? The previous moment does not determine your future; it's your judgment about the previous moment that determines your future. So when negativity or ignorance arise, just brush them off with a smile, knowing that such moments offer you a fresh opportunity to get back on track to becoming authentically alive.

Ground yourself in the intention to be radically alive. I like these words of Dr. Howard Thurman: "Don't worry about what the world needs. Ask yourself what makes you come alive, and do that. Because what the world needs is people who have come alive."[3] This means that, as long as you are on the planet, you are here to deliver your gifts, your talents, and your skills with confidence and inner authority, withholding nothing. This is when you are living full out, moving in the reality of love, affluence, and artistry of being. Your radical aliveness not only affects your individual life but life on the planet as we know it.

### REALITY TRAINING

As has been emphasized, the questions that we ask ourselves on a regular basis are very important. When we ask the ultimate question, "What is real?" the faculty that allows us to see the invisible is activated. Our intuition begins to offer bursts of direct knowing. You may be led to a teacher, to a spiritual practice that will begin to unlock the mysteries of existence for you, or you may become so committed to living in the "now" moment that all questioning ceases except how you may become a beneficial presence on the planet.

Each of us is in reality training. The length of time it takes for us to wake up to the Real is our own responsibility. There is no external force that judges, rewards, or interferes with our awakening, but the longer we postpone, the longer we delay our joy. The sooner we surrender to the lead of the Self, the sooner we enter the realm of the Real. Remember, no outside source is bestowing anything upon you, nor is there a godhead to supplicate, to give you a special grace to shorten your training. There is no God to please, appease, or displease because the Spirit has already given you all that you require for the journey. You are already in the temple which requires that you bow down to nothing except the divinity of your own being. Jesus never knelt down before a cross, Buddha never bowed to a statue, and Krishna never worshipped an external deity.

You are a conscious magnetic field capable of drawing to yourself all that is required to successfully train in Reality consciousness. The purpose of your training is to wake up to the outer and inner harmony of the universe in spite of all appearances to the contrary. What will be left to complain about once you have tasted such nirvana? So enter your training wholeheartedly. Take a concentrated dose of the Real and awaken to the beauty that is You. Train in being gracious enough to receive it, to reveal it, to radiate it.

By whatever path, once you arrive at a superconscious realization of Reality, all maps are tossed aside. They are no longer required because from that point on the journey is uncharted.

### Affirmation

*On the ground where I now stand, I declare my aliveness, my sensitivity to the Good that surrounds and infiltrates me.*
*I live authentically, ever attuned to intuitive guidance from within that expresses through me as originality, creativity, harmony, and wholeness.*

### Embodiment

I give my consent to living my life as a work of art in communion with the Real. I no longer give credence to the external world's actuarial tables, statistics, or percentages. I am a free agent of my own destiny. My body temple, my emotional body, the body of my affairs is shot through with limitless creativity, and this creativity is the artistic order of my days.

I realize that behind every human aberration there is a spiritual aspiration endeavoring to break into expression. I call this forth within myself, knowing absolutely that my inner being contains all that is needed to reveal the beauty of my infinite nature.

I am in service to Infinite Beauty, Infinite Compassion, Infinite Love. My eyes, ears, and all my senses are in service to the Most High. No longer caught in a loop of emotional turmoil or self-judgment, I sense the pattern of wholeness that underlies all life. With an artist's perceptivity, I know and sense this truth throughout my entire being.

No one determines my destiny. Neither circumstance, history, DNA, past or future anxiety, fluctuations in the world's economy—none of this determines my destiny. With each breath I become more myself. This declaration is made in my consciousness of the Real, liberating me from any thoughts of lack, limitation, or separation from my Good. All of my needs are met. Well-being, strength, vitality, opulence, joy, creativity, wisdom, enthusiasm, artistic perceptivity, spiritual discernment—these qualities vibrate through my consciousness. My conscious mind, subconscious mind, and superconscious mind embody this truth that I speak. I decree that unconditional love is shot through all of my relationships and expresses as lovingkindness, compassion, and forgiveness. As an artist, as a beholder of the real, as a spiritual discerner, I am conscious of all that I think, say, and do.

I wholeheartedly enter Reality training. I am a worthy and magnificent student and know that I am a candidate for enlightenment. As a spiritual being having a human incarnation, I choose Reality as a conscious function of my awareness. Every organ and function of my body temple accepts this truth. Every thought form is receptive to it. My subconscious and conscious minds are aligned in agreement and my superconscious mind is empowered. I sense and know my oneness with the dynamic, harmonizing Presence of the Ineffable, and the universe reflects back to me the truth of this embodiment. I humbly give thanks knowing that factual evidence is given to my faith.

## Notes

1. H. Inayat Khan, *The Mysticism of Sound and Music: Music, the Power of the Word, Cosmic Language* (Boston: Shambhala Publications, Inc., 1991).
2. John 14:12.
3. Howard Thurman, *For the Inward Journey: The Writings of Howard Thurman* (Richmond, Ind.: Friends United Press, 1984).

# 11

# Jesus the Christ:
## Master of the Existential Encounter

---

*Mother, Father, God, how great thou art*
*How infinite, how wonderful*
*So very close, so very near*
*My breath begins and ends with you*

Call it the "second coming" if you'd like to, but the truth is it's here now. Think about it: How can it come back if it has never gone away? The Christ Intelligence interpenetrates every speck of cosmic creation and all beings. It is not the Christ that has gone away from us; rather, we have not expanded our consciousness to realize the super-truth of our own Christed state of consciousness. The second coming occurs when we awaken to our own state of Christ consciousness.

Jesus said, "The harvest truly is plenteous, but the laborers are few."[1] It's as though the Universe were advertising his message on its cosmic radio station:

> *"Knock, and it shall be opened to you."*[2]
> Dear listeners, this guarantee is backed by enlightened
> beings who have time-tested this 2,000-year-old product.
> They knocked, and heavenly realizations opened to

> them. So take advantage of this offer now by investing the spiritual coin of your commitment to being a skilled laborer in the field of ever-evolving consciousness.

Are you willing to commit to following Jesus' example and inwardly practice as he did? His state of Christ consciousness was not ready-made; he worked for it through his spiritual practices of meditation, prayer, contemplation, introspection, and solitary retreats. He was Jesus the man who became Jesus the Christ; the same Christ that each of us is when we become self-realized.

## THE EVERYDAY EXISTENTIAL ENCOUNTER

We have encounters throughout any given day, so what is it that designates most of them as being ordinary from one that may be defined as existential?

An existential encounter is about encountering or seeing the Christ in oneself and others. Thomas Merton, the awakened Trappist monk, put it so beautifully when he described his own existential encounter, "Then it was as if I suddenly saw the secret beauty of their hearts, the depths of their hearts where neither sin nor desire nor self-knowledge can reach, the core of their reality, the person that each one is in the eyes of the Divine. If only they could all see themselves as they really are. If only we could see each other that way all the time. There would be no more war, no more hatred, no more cruelty, no more greed ... I suppose the big problem would be that we would fall down and worship each other."[3]

Jesus was a master of the existential encounter. He saw perfect spiritual virtue where the crowd saw an adulteress. He saw perfect health in the physically afflicted when he told the lame to walk, commanded withered limbs to be made whole, the blind to see. When others saw a lack of food, he saw an abundance of loaves and fishes. When Lazarus was lying seemingly lifeless before Jesus, he regenerated the life force of the living spirit in which he beheld his dear friend.

What you encounter in your daily life, no matter how simple, may also be experienced as an existential encounter. If you are a sculptor, you will see in the marble the prefect image that is to emerge. If you are a songwriter, you will hear with the inner ear the perfect words to complement a melody. If you are a parent, you will see the highest potential within your child even in the midst of misbehavior. If you are a spiritual practitioner, you will see the perfect spiritual being in the midst of the neuroses and pathology of others and yourself.

An existential encounter is determined, then, by where we place our attention and the inner response we experience to what we "see." As we look out upon our world, we may feel that we don't see evidence of the greatness that lives within each individual. Christlike love seems hard to come by, even from those who profess to follow the teachings of Jesus the Christ in whose name intolerance, bigotry, exclucivity, war, and crimes against humanity have been practiced down through the ages.

We may wonder what has happened to Jesus' teaching, "By this all will know that you are my disciples, if you have love for one another."[4] This couples with his asking, in substance, how can we love God, whom we can't see, if we don't love our brothers and sisters whom we can see? Christian mystic Howard Thurman said that love is to meet a person where they are in consciousness, but to treat them as though their spiritual potential were actualized. Imagine how such an approach would bring out the best in people.

When we have a spiritual orientation towards life, we will see the beauty that surrounds us, the perfect man, woman, and child that shines the light of the Christ-self.

I'm reminded of when Dr. Robert Thurman, professor of Indo-Tibetan Studies at Columbia and author of *Why the Dalai Lama Matters*, spoke at my spiritual center. He described how the Dalai Lama sees the good in the people of China, how he prays for their highest welfare and wishes them to thrive, even as he witnesses the massacre of his people and the recent beatings during protests that took place in Burma and for which the Chinese government blamed him. His was an existential encounter with those who the world called his enemies.

**THE CHRIST-ENERGY IS FULLY OPERATIVE IN OUR WORLD**

The Christ-energy is fully present in our world. It was not manifest on the planet only during a specific time or only when a specific awakened being walked the planet.

There are among us today individuals who practice Christ-like love. Dr. A. T. Ariyaratne of Sri Lanka walks with his "soldiers" directly and silently through the spray of bullets in civil wars. During 9/11, Katrina, and other disasters, many individuals sacrificed their lives so that others could live. "Greater love has no one than this, than to lay down one's life for his friends," Jesus said.[5] When Saint Francis had his existential encounter, wolves came and sat at his feet. Gandhi could not bear to walk on the grass because he felt it groan under his feet. Tigers became as tame as house cats in the presence of the Buddha.

Those of us living in the twenty-first century are fully qualified to experience our own existential encounter and live the Christ-ideals of unconditional love, forgiveness, and God-consciousness. When we embody the ways of a peacemaker, we put down our sword of aggression in our thoughts, speech, and actions, and we say, along with the Dalai Lama, that our religion is kindness, which encompasses compassion, forgiveness, peace, and joy.

## THE LUMINOSITY OF BEING

Jesus taught, "If thine eye be single, thy whole body will be full of light."[6] Metaphysically, he was informing us that by keeping our inner eye—the eye of the soul—single, we too may have an existential encounter.

How do we deep our eye single? By communing with the light-energy of the Christ consciousness within us. We keep our eye single when, in meditation, we close our two eyes and gently place our focus on the third eye, located in the middle of the forehead. When our two eyes become single, we realize that the body temple is indeed a portable home of our soul-force. As we see this within ourselves, we understand that this inner light resides within all beings. Then, when we encounter others, we can practice seeing this "light that lighteth up every man that cometh into the world."[7]

This is the single eye to which Jesus referred. In Sanskrit, it is called the *Kutastha Chaitanya*, the *ajna* chakra. Five thousand years ago, the rishis of India passed down techniques to their students for seeing this third eye that are practiced to this day.

You will find it a very centering experience to gently, without straining or crossing your eyes, place your awareness at this point between the eyebrows during meditation and interior prayer. Experiment in the laboratory of your own consciousness and develop your own 20/20 inner vision.

## YOUR BODY IS NOT SOLID MATTER

Through his resurrection, Jesus proved that the physical body is part of a field of cosmic energy; it is not solid matter. In his Christ-conscious state, he had mastery over the physical realm and was able to command the atoms of his body to reconstruct themselves, to raise Lazarus from the dead, and to perform many healings. By walking on water, he proved that it is possible to change the vibratory rate of the body, making it lighter than other elements. Yogis and fakirs in India walk through walls, levitate, and bury themselves under the earth for weeks at a time, living directly from the *prana*, the life force or life-energy that sustains creation.

Spiritually illumined beings display their powers not to extol themselves, but to reveal the unseen reality of life that it might arouse our spiritual interest and inquiry, settle our doubts, encourage us to realize that the same potential lies within our consciousness if we do the inner work. Quantum physics is catching up with what has been realized by spiritual masters throughout the ages: we are electromagnetic waves of energy housed in bodily form.

## A MOST PRACTICAL WAY TO LIVE

Jesus encouraged us to pray in solitariness, saying, "When you pray, go into your room, and when you have shut your door, pray to your Father who is in the secret place."[8] Through this spiritual instruction, he is encouraging us to make time to set aside the cares of everyday life, shut the door of our five outward senses, and commune with the Spirit in "secret," meaning in the secret-soul of consciousness. (We may also follow his example and occasionally take a retreat where we may devote even more time to our inner practices.) At first, we experience an uplifted awareness more deeply when meditating, but the time comes when we are able to live, move, and have our being in the after-effects of meditation. The results of our practice are most clearly revealed when we leave our meditation seat and engage with the world.

Although it may not at first seem like it, *living as an awakened being is the most practical way to live.* In our infotainment-saturated society, this may sound quite unappealing, boring, or even frightening. It's practically impossible today to go to the car wash, a restaurant, airports, medical appointments, or even some public restrooms without having a television in the room lest we have spaces of time, vacancies that alert us that they must be filled. Meditation may seem like something from another planet or something that can only be done when life's many demands slow down. But again I say that *being spiritually awake is the most practical way to live.* It is then that we may live as Jesus did by not worrying "about your life, what you will eat or what you will drink; nor about your body, what you will put on. Is not life more than food and the body more than clothing? Look at the birds of the air, for they neither sow nor reap nor gather into barns yet your Heavenly Father feeds them. Are you not of more value than they?"[9]

This does not mean that we ignore our worldly responsibilities or that we don't get our physical needs or those of our family met. Nor does it mean we forget about abundance and beauty. If Jesus walked the earth with us now, he would no doubt adapt aspects of his teaching to meet the needs of twenty-first-century living, but without diluting the heart of his teaching to "seek ye first the kingdom of God and his righteousness and all these things will be added unto you," which is an anxiety-free way to live.[10] A new New Testament would be written. Jesus realized that the most practical way to live was to put God first, to make meditation and prayer our first activity of the day, to place our trust in the changeless Spirit so that, as we experience the inevitable vicissitudes of life, we navigate them with absolute trust in the fundamental goodness of the universe.

## WHAT CONSTITUTES MEDITATION

Meditation is the application of a technique that teaches how to place undistracted attention on the Real. While activities such as exercise, yoga, listening to music, and experiencing the beauty in the arts are inspiring, they are not substitutes for meditation. "Be still and know that I am God" means that we must enter the silence long enough to catch spiritual insights and to hear the still, small voice of intuition speaking within, guiding us, nurturing us, making us mindful of where we place our consciousness throughout the day.[11]

## THE ANGEL OF CHANGE

I'd like to introduce you to an energy dynamic I call the "angel of change." This energetic is more like a devil to individuals who resist change. The egoic structure of the little self balks; it wants to stay the same so that it may retain the illusion of control over the external world, including other people and circumstances.

Challenging circumstances are the calling card of the angel of change. They serve to loosen our octopus grip on limited thinking; they shift our everyday reference points, creating a gap through which Reality may enter our awareness. When we resist change, the angel of change seems negative and may even invade our dream state causing us to have nightmares. When we surrender and give our consent to the changes that we are guided to make, the angel of change appears as a benevolent, kind, caring energy. Then, instead of nightmares, we have dreams of well-being and inner initiations.

## IGNITE A FIRE OF DESIRE WITHIN YOURSELF

The common denominator among all the enlightened ones is that they were filled with the fire from heaven, burning with the desire to consciously commune with Reality. Mahatma Gandhi's quality of Christ consciousness was that of a peace that surpassed human understanding. His spiritual awakening became the conduit for the emancipation of India. George Washington Carver saw the face of Spirit peering back at him through the flowers and plants. His great love caused them to yield their secrets to him. Follow the example of the Great Ones! Ignite a fire of desire to realize your own Buddhahood, your own Christhood.

Begin by centering yourself in meditation and asking your higher Self what qualities you are to cultivate. Listen deeply as your inner spirit speaks within your own heart. Next, make that soul-quality come alive and be real to you. You may even want to record your own voice claiming ownership of this quality. Maybe add music in the background that you feel energetically vibrates in harmony with the quality you have chosen. Listen to it in your car, when performing routine tasks, and when you fall asleep at night. This will energize your magnetic field for drawing to you what is required to support you in the cultivation of your soul-qualities.

Deliberately pause at intervals throughout your day's activities and check in with yourself. For example, let's say that you have chosen the quality of compassion. Experiment with this simple exercise. Gently close your eyes. Breathe in a long inhalation and slowly exhale. Gently ask within, "Right here and right now, do I feel a vibration of compassion flowing within my consciousness?" If not, ask your inner Self to open and reveal the compassion that is part and parcel of your true nature. As you attune with the vibration of compassion, merge your whole awareness into it, feeling all of its textures. Imagine it filling every fiber of your being. Amplify it, then relax.

Observe without judgment how you walk through your daily activities. Throughout your day, pause to ask yourself, "Where is my consciousness?" When driving to work in heavy traffic, notice if you are impatient or if you have compassion for the other drivers who also want to arrive at their destination on time. Look for opportunities to practice your chosen quality. Are you mindfully present in the moment? Remember that during challenging moments, you may turn to the authority within your own mind and say, "This does not move me! I have unshakable faith in the Infinite Presence right within me and all around me."

Why does this simple technique work? Because when you set your intention and remain unswervingly faithful to it, evidence emerges in your experience that your chosen quality has been within you all along. How else could it come into expression if it didn't already exist in your spiritual DNA? When you act in faith, believing that the quality of the Spirit you have chosen to cultivate already exists within the fabric of your true nature, the law of mental equivalents moves upon your conviction and reveals it in your outer experience.

When you awaken each morning, instead of jumping out of bed, briefly pause. Smile in grateful acknowledgment and acceptance of your life exactly as it is. Then meditate, if only for ten minutes. Continue to pause throughout the day to notice where your consciousness is hanging out. At the end of each day, make it a part of your spiritual practice to introspect. Without judgment and with great kindness, be honest with yourself.

Meditate, pray, serve, study, and smile. Know that your life is carried in the palm of God's hand.

### Affirmation

*I welcome an existential encounter into my life and even now prepare my consciousness through meditation, affirmative prayer, contemplation, and introspection.*

*I am open, receptive, pliable, and teachable. I move into my Christed state of consciousness.*

## Embodiment

I speak this word with absolute authority from the depths of my faith, from my utter trust in the power and presence of God. I know that this presence is more than law and principle. It is real! It is alive and lives within my own consciousness, calling me to open myself to its fullness. I may have been sleeping, but no longer can I ignore the knock of the Spirit at the door of my heart. Surrounded with divine love, peace, joy, and transforming knowledge, I surrender. I am willing to enter an existential encounter with myself. The veils of ignorance are parting and glimmers of the light of the truth of being are infiltrating my awareness. A divine knowingness that I stand at the center of Reality is ignited within my consciousness.

Anything from my past of a moment ago that would hinder my awakening has returned to the nothingness from which it came. I do not have to coerce enlightenment to occur, I have only to welcome it, and I do so now. False fear that my life will never be the same, that I will have to sacrifice that which I hold dear no longer holds sway over me. I open myself to a realization of unbroken communion with Reality, with the Christ consciousness of my true nature.

When the Spirit created me in its own image and likeness and named it me, I know this was not a meaningless act. I am intentional; I am on purpose, and from this moment on, I treat myself in the light of this truth. I treat others in the light of this truth, knowing that they too are emanations of the Spirit of Life.

I break any old agreements I have made—knowingly and unknowingly—with mediocrity. I have a new realization of who and what I really am. I have a new sense of my oneness with my Oversoul. I join with all beings who have gone before me and awakened to their true nature. I call on my teachers and guides in this realm and in the invisible realm and know that I am divinely supported by them. They cheer me on as I now consciously rise in consciousness and accept the mantle of enlightened living. Though I may stumble and fall, I know that this universe mothers me, that I am held on the lap of infinite compassion, infinite patience, infinite unconditional love. So it is easy for me to forgive myself for any missteps. It is easy for me to realign, re-attune myself to my spiritual intentions to live and love as did Jesus the Christ, as did the Buddha, as have all the saints and sages. I know that I am as loved and cherished by the Ineffable as they are.

I surrender any mental habit patterns that would deny this, my statement of what is now real in my life. I accept myself the way that God sees me—with a sincere, pure desire to know who and what I really am. I feel it now. I feel my luminosity of being and I bow before it with great gratitude. For this and so much more, I am so grateful.

And in the energy of this word, I include all sentient beings. May all hearts be comforted, may all be fed with physical and divine nourishment. May peace fill all hearts and the planet. I know it is done and I simply say, thank you.

## Notes

1. Matthew 9:37.
2. Matthew 7:7.
3. Thomas Merton, *Conjectures of a Guilty Bystander* (New York: Doubleday, 1966).
4. John 13:35.
5. John 15:13.
6. Matthew 6:22.
7. John 1:9.
8. Matthew 6:6.
9. Matthew 6:25–26.
10. Matthew 6:33.
11. Psalm 46:10.

# 12
# The Myth of Perfection

*In the land of I AM, I am*
*More than I will be, I am*
*All that I AM*
*You can't fall from grace in the Land*
*You cannot be hurt in the Land*

Are you waiting for your perfect job, perfect mate, perfect children, perfect weight, perfect car, perfect home, perfect spiritual path—an overall perfected self before you give yourself the gift of self-acceptance? If so, you are setting yourself up for disappointment. No matter how many credentials, accolades, wall plaques, or trophies you acquire, your jubilation will be cut short by a rude intruder: the ego's gossip that you aren't yet quite eligible for self-acceptance without just a little stronger sense of your self-importance.

The myth of perfection is widely taught and believed in. People feel unacceptable to themselves until they live up to their own or others' definitions of what it means to be perfect. Most people have never even examined those definitions in order to dispel their mythology. And no matter how well we live up to them, if we have not created a welcome home in our hearts for ourselves, we will not be comfortable in our own skin. As long as we believe that until we accumulate enough outer evidence of having arrived at the "good life," we prevent ourselves from relaxing into self-acceptance.

Baby boomers—people born between 1946 and 1964—were raised eating a cereal that was branded as "the breakfast of champions," which came packaged in boxes with photos of Olympic gold medalists and other idealized role models. The obvious message was, "These people are perfect. They eat our cereal, and if you eat it too, you can become perfect." We have taken over where our parents, educators, coaches, religious leaders, and society have left off in our perfection-training.

Perfection and a standard of excellence both require commitment, discipline, and one-pointedness. However, they differ in their motives and results: *A perfectionist must outstrip the competition and satisfy the ego. A person who functions at a standard of excellence reflects his or her personal best while satisfying the heart. Those seeking perfection push others aside for the sake of personal gain. Those who strive for excellence seek success for others as well as themselves.*

## YOUR PERFECTLY IMPERFECT SELF

Constantly tinkering with whatever we believe our imperfections are can overtake our lives. Look at what's happening to our children today as they compete to get into a college while they're still in middle school! "Whatever it takes" is our national mantra. Government programs, such as No Child Left Behind, force our teachers to become consummate test givers and our children robotic test takers, memorizing rather than learning, so that they may do well on standardized tests. Parents, fearful that their children will not get into the college of their choice, push them so hard that children are sleep deprived, play deprived, exercise deprived, artistically deprived.

Never before in our history has there been such a high suicide rate among teenagers. Seldom do they have a moment alone to get to know themselves, to discover their innate creativity. They have no time for anything other than competing to make it in what they are taught is an unfriendly, cold, competitive world. Instead of discovering their natural talents, gifts, and skills, they are programmed for conformity and capitulation to a world outside of themselves. I recently read a newspaper ad encouraging parents to send in photos of their kids to have any physical flaws airbrushed to perfection. This sends a message to children that they aren't pretty or handsome enough just as they are. What insanity! How can parents who have not learned to accept themselves raise children who are self-accepting? When children are taught the truth about their inherent riches, our world will be much less impoverished.

## YOU'RE ALL RIGHT ALREADY

Sometimes we hesitate to accept ourselves as we are because we are concerned that we will fall into complacency, become lazy, and stop striving to grow into our full potential. This misunderstanding comes from the philosophy of "don't rest on your laurels." The core message says, "You're still not perfect enough, not quite 'there' yet, so don't stop to appreciate yourself because you might settle for your current state of development." Self-acceptance does not mean that we give up our intention to expand, excel, and grow. *Self-acceptance, which is independent of the praise from the outside world, accelerates our potential for growth because it nurtures us from within. It is motivation of the self by the Self.*

Accepting our perfectly imperfect self is an inside job. It cannot be postponed until we are convinced that we are living up to our own or someone else's definition of neurotic perfection. Let us instead strive to live in a state of radical self-acceptance. We can do this despite the convoluted notions of the ego. Give yourself some space. The universe cuts us some slack called "grace." When you get wound up in a sense of unworthiness, guilt, shame, and embarrassment about being you as you are you, give yourself some grace with this reminder, "I'm all right already." Then breathe.

When you seek a spiritual path because it will "fix" you, it then becomes just another gimmick, a medicine to cure what ails you, to shut up the ego's voice that nags you, that's always whispering, "You're not all right." This is how the ego succeeds in running its favorite racket of keeping you constantly tinkering with yourself, so engaged in your ego that you don't move into an awareness of your already inherent wholeness. It keeps you living in a state of duality. If you continue listening to the ego, you can take up an entire lifetime of working on yourself to achieve some imaginary outer perfection. You will live in polarity, constantly pitting the "good" self against the "bad" self. This is hellish living. It is a no win situation, and you will never be at peace. An authentic spiritual path will always give you back to yourself by providing the tools for self-realization, for self-empowerment.

When you move through life in a consciousness of "I'm all right already," you realize that you aren't moving from a state of imperfection to perfection, from incompletion to completion. Instead, you understand that you are moving from one point of development to the next. Then angst transmutes into the relaxation of self-acceptance, of getting off your case and moving on.

Here is a remedy for the ego's confusion: instead of looking for outer perfection, look within at the true nature of the Self, which is patterned after perfection itself. Stop wasting your time creating a façade of outer perfection whose falsity is subject to being shattered, revealed at any moment. As the revered Hindu sage Sri Aurobindo wisely taught, "There can be no real perfection for us except by our inner self."[1] This inner Self is already perfect, regardless of what is happening on the outer side of life.

The word *radical* comes from the Latin *radix*, meaning "going to the origin, root, source." When we turn within to the origin of the Self, we will realize the true nature of perfection and know that we are all right already.

### RE-LANDSCAPING YOUR GARDEN OF EDEN CONSCIOUSNESS

Perhaps you've been indoctrinated into the belief that you were conceived and born in original sin, that you were flawed from the get-go and require a master gardener to eradicate the weeds of sinfulness from your inner Garden of Eden. There is only one "original sin," and that is the "original ignorance" of a belief that you are separate from the Whole, from your Source. Sri Aurobindo describes it as "the deviation from the Truth and Right of the Spirit, from its oneness, integrality and harmony."[2] When we remove the debris of original ignorance from our pristine Eden consciousness of Oneness, of Wholeness, we experience our inner riches. The good news is that it's never too late to dispel the ego's illusion of separation and once again walk freely in the exquisite garden of our being.

It is entirely within your capacity to reenter your original state of basic innocence—before your conditioning by outside influences. You may begin right now by investing a little time to contemplate the following: What is your definition of perfection? What behaviors are a result of your definition? Do they create peace, intelligence, happiness? What are the sources of your definition? Do you still agree with them? What is your definition of self-acceptance? In what ways do you practice self-affirmation?

Are you able to give yourself genuine encouragement when you are in the midst of a challenge?

Then, as you go about your day, stop and ask yourself, "How am I relating to myself in this circumstance? In this moment, do I accept myself?"

Self-acceptance greatly depends on our trust in the fundamental goodness of the universe, the same fundamental goodness that is within us. Discovering and living from this awareness redeems us from the myth of outer perfection and from the need to be saved by someone or something outside of ourselves. It gives us the understanding that behind every human aberration there is a human aspiration. That aspiration is to realize the Authentic Self, which has nothing to do with outer perfection.

### STABILIZING YOUR LIFE STRUCTURES

The central confusion lies in the ego's drive for outer perfection while the core Self seeks to express its inner perfection. Many people write to me asking what they're doing wrong when the law of manifestation doesn't deliver their desired style of life once they've calibrated the "if you can imagine it, you can have it" mind-set. The universe is not concerned with whether or not we have the top ten symbols that announce to ourselves and to the world that we have "made it." This type of material achievement is not the sign of our spiritual attainment as spiritual materialists would have us believe.

As you will gather from the overall tenor of this book's message, I teach the application of the law of manifestation so that we may stabilize our basic life structures. It is beneficial to be financially stable so that we are not distracted by worries about finances and so that our energy may be directed to cultivating consciousness. We are to use the laws of manifestation where health is concerned so that our body temple is not an obstacle to our spiritual practices such as meditation, contemplation, visioning, or a impediment to sharing our gifts and talents with the world. We are to align ourselves with the universal laws so that we experience relationships that are harmonious, that are a source of mutual growth. However, this is not spiritual materialism; it is a conscious and wise application of the law of manifestation.

## OUTWITTING THE EGO'S RACKETS

The ego-mind looks at our personalities, physical appearance, homes, mates, and careers as indicators that we've made it. The ego's motivator, its cheerleader, is exaggerated self-criticism interspersed with waving pom-poms of "you did it, you hot thing you!" When we are anchored in a consciousness of our true nature, we live unaffected by false self-importance, false humility, false superiority, or false inferiority. We govern our lives with wisdom, compassion, dignity, equanimity, joy—the spirit-qualities inherent within us. It is entirely possible to live in such a consciousness.

This does not mean that we will have perfectly charming personalities and never irritate anyone or that we will never make a mistake. It means we will have loving compassion for ourselves, which provides the encouragement to grow, to continue our walk toward awakening. And we will extend these same qualities to others.

How do you see yourself as currently governing your life? What are the laws of your inner being? Is it harmonious to live inside of You?

## STRETCH INTO YOUR AUTHENTIC SELF

If you've ever practiced yoga *asanas* you know that as you gently, properly stretch the muscles you eventually become more flexible and your performance of the asanas improves. In yoga practice, the body eliminates tension and toxins from the muscles and vital organs. In the same way, as we stretch into our Authentic Self, we will relax more deeply into our fundamental ground of being and eliminate the toxins of ego that convince us we will be hurt by not following its direction. The ego contracts in the face of the unknown, releasing toxins of inner conflict and fear. With trust in the goodness of Existence comes flexibility and openness, which eliminates the toxin of self-doubt and makes room for trust and love of the Authentic Self. Osho put it beautifully: "This Existence is ready to support you in every possible way. Trust, and you will feel a new upsurge of energy in you. That energy is love."[3]

*You don't have to develop trust and love because they already exist within your inner treasure house. Discover them!* As you stretch your awareness and realize how you are cherished by the Ineffable, you will know that you are, always have been, and always will be divinely supported in your journey into self-love, self-appreciation, self-respect, self-realization. An alchemical change will begin to occur on subtle levels of being, and you will reveal more of yourself than a moment ago. You have not literally transformed—you have cleansed the obscurations covering your organic goodness. You have discarded a layer of your mental armor—mental conditioning—that obscures your vision of yourself as the exquisite being that you are. You are not creating perfection; you uncover, discover, and express your innate wholeness.

## HAVE A DEEPER CONVERSATION WITH YOURSELF

If you've kept any old journals and occasionally read them, you will see how experience constantly breaks up into change. Very often, the things about which we experience fear, worry, and doubt never even came to pass. Unless we invest our energy in negative emotions by latching on to them, they will pass through the sky of our mind. These emotions feel very visceral when they are flowing through us because we haven't been taught the skillful means for witnessing them without becoming involved in them. We grasp the thoughts we like and try to disown the ones we don't like, hiding them from ourselves and certainly from others. *In fact, our attempt at outer perfection is a major hiding place, a way to avoid ourselves.*

Have a deeper conversation with yourself about how you relate to the temporary clouds passing through the sky of your mind, to the Self that witnesses them. Witnessing our thoughts is a skillful means by which we learn to take a more impersonal, objective view of our neurotic tendencies with an attitude of, "Oh, there's an interesting one." We can actually develop a sense of humor about our foibles.

We want to consistently express the qualities we are praised for and suppress and repress qualities we are criticized for so that people will like us. *How can we ever know peace in a mental household divided against itself?* We must break the habit of subconscious gossip by opening our hearts to ourselves in genuine self-friendship and compassion. The heart is very wise, and when you enter the beauty of its inner chamber you will relax into your fundamental state of well-being.

### DON'T BITE THE BAIT

When you read autobiographies or biographies of individuals and spiritual giants the world deeply admires, you will note that it is not unusual for their outer personalities to be challenging, eccentric, difficult to deal with. They are not interested in society's definitions of "pleasing personalities." What they have done is tap into the deep roots of being and share their enlightening insights in a way that changes lives and ultimately uplifts the planet.

Personality is a façade we create to interact with the world; it is the persona we shine up and present to the public. Our personality is created by influences outside of ourselves, the conditioning we have received to make ourselves socially acceptable. It is another layer of armor we must break through in order to have genuine self-discovery. It takes great courage to inquire into the reality of being, to sincerely want to get to know ourselves through and through. It is the inner work of the spiritual warrior.

By not biting the bait of societal myths about perfection, you will reveal your own unique character. Your energy will be invested in expressing your soul qualities and allowing them to inform your outer life. Then you will discover something wonderful is happening: in the stillness of your communion with your-Self, you will watch the clouds of thoughts pass through and realize that you have not only stepped out of your past personal history, you have also stopped projecting into the future. *You will be present to the timeless dimension of now.* You will realize self-love and self-appreciation without inhibition or self-consciousness about doing so. Your insights will be fresh, new. This is the Universe giving you feedback that you are becoming spiritually mature and living more from your true nature. New openings, new insights will go on revealing themselves. You will think that you have changed, but it is not so. You have stripped away more of what obscures your Essential Self. This begins the adventure of being you as you are you, of loving yourself as you are you.

## FULL SELF-ESTEEM AHEAD!

So often we confuse self-esteem with a healthy ego—healthy in the sense of "inflated." Self-esteem really means self-respect, and self-respect is a product of knowing who and what we really are as a spiritual being having a human incarnation. As was stated earlier, the road to that realization is lighted by trust and love. It is important to let go of excuses such as, "Oh, one of these days, when I no longer have to deal with a bad boss, an incompatible mate, my delinquent child, I'll get it together." The truth is that right in the midst of whatever you feel stuck in you can trust yourself, you can love yourself through it. It is only a breath away when you know that your true happiness is independent of any circumstance in which you find yourself. When this realization is birthed in your consciousness, you will live in heaven, even as you are planted firmly on the Earth. You will join heaven and earth.

There is a well-known story about a Samurai warrior who wanted to know the difference between heavenly and hellish states of being. One day he approached his teacher, saying, "Master, please, may I have your teachings on the difference between living in the hell realm and the heaven realm?" Feigning anger, the teacher said, "Get away from me! You are ignorant, stupid! Why would I waste my time teaching you anything? Stop wasting my time and get out of here!" Upon hearing his teacher's harsh words, the Samurai warrior's ego was so insulted that he pulled out his sword with the intent to cut off the master's head. Just as he began to swing, the master began to laugh saying, "That, my son, is hell." The warrior-student was so moved by his teacher's willingness to risk his own life to give him this precious teaching that he became overwhelmed with respect and humility. All he could say was, "Please, Rinpoche, accept my utmost gratitude," to which the master responded, "Ahhh, now that is heaven."

So another skillful means to realize self-esteem is to be grateful that life brings to us all that we require to wake up. Success and what we label as failure are both part of our journey; they are equally vital to our growth. This includes the painful experiences we would prefer to push away—the pain of loss, unrequited love, thwarted ambitions, even the pain of awakening. Our willingness to look life straight in the eye, to unmask ourselves and drop our pretensions, illusions, disappointments, and hurts, says, "Thank you for breaking yet another one of my illusions so that I may become free!" *We discover within ourselves the humility to be a beginner over and over again, which keeps us teachable.*

## WHO SAID, "YOU'RE ONLY HUMAN"?

As we open our hearts, we will see that our individual challenges and those our planet is facing come from the reactive mind. Justifications such as, "I didn't really want to do it, but I'm only human, so I hit him;" or, "We suspect that they are planning to bomb us, so a preemptive strike is the only possible response," are the ego's desire to maintain control and thereby survive at all costs. The notion that "I'm only human" becomes an excuse for revenge, hatred, violence, injustice, laziness. Once this excuse is imprinted in our subconscious, we begin to operate from that mind-set of self-preservation, which in turn becomes a breeding ground for selfishness, greed, retaliation, lack of forgiveness. The law of self-preservation is the law of the unaware, unawakened human experience. What exactly is preserved? The ego, and its sense of an existence separate from the Whole.

The false rationale that "I'm only human" is to be replaced with this: "I am a spiritual being having a precious human incarnation. I have the innate capacity to reveal my true nature of wholeness, wisdom, joy, peace, compassion. I keep this truth about myself before my inner gaze, and I know this to be the truth about all beings. In a consciousness of love and gratitude, I allow my oneness with the Whole to inform my thoughts and actions."

By single-mindedly keeping the truth about ourselves and all beings before us, we don't so readily describe ourselves as being "only human," thereby justifying aggression and violence against others and ourselves. Instead, we remind ourselves that we may bring the light of wisdom, compassion, unconditional love, forgiveness, generosity of heart, self-acceptance, and trust into our relationship with ourselves and others.

## JOINING HEAVEN AND EARTH

The emphasis on activating the inner side of life doesn't mean that we deny the everyday responsibilities and joys of being human. Not at all. We are not here to be of no earthly good or to deny the delight of human experiences. Life in its juiciness, its passion, is beautiful. We don't need to become self-sacrificing ascetics living in a cave or isolated in our home in order to become self-realized.

Many years ago, when I wanted to prove my love for God and my commitment to search for enlightenment, I thought about becoming a monk. Fortunately, a teacher of mine wisely said, "If you sacrifice life, you sacrifice God. You need to be joined with the continent of life, rooted in it." I have followed that instruction and can say from experience that it is a powerful way of trusting life, trusting the Whole of existence, and trusting oneself. Our incarnation is safe and secure, regardless of outer appearances. Only the ego is insecure.

Begin conducting life from your true nature of Oneness, of Wholeness, rather than from the reactive human ego, which is concerned primarily with itself. As we matriculate through Earth school, we have the opportunity to expand our consciousness, to become intimately acquainted with Spirit, to open ourselves in complete vulnerability to its unconditional love for us, to its blessings and grace that unceasingly seek us out. When we open ourselves to receive these gifts, our hearts become softened, and it becomes easier for the ego to surrender its relentless drive for human perfection. Lao-tzu encourages us to "Surrender to life. Allow life to lead you, don't try to lead life. Don't try to manipulate and control life. Let life possess you. You simply surrender. You give total power to life, and be with it."[4] Surrender in this sense is not about acquiescing to a God or deity outside of ourselves; it is about yielding to the Spirit becoming conscious of itself in, through, and as us.

The ego resists because it is afraid it will lose its influence over you. Just remember that a bad day for your ego is a good day for your soul. Surrender is a courageous action in and of itself. When surrender informs our thoughts and actions, we walk in harmony and peace.

### LOVE, LOVER, AND BELOVED

Love starts with self-love. Acceptance starts with self-acceptance. Compassion begins with self-compassion. Surrender starts with self-surrender. These are the avenues through which we open ourselves to sharing our love, compassion, and wisdom with our loved ones, with our community, with our world. The longing we feel inside for that "missing something" gets misconstrued into a lack of material things, emotional needs, egoic needs—when all along the deepest desire of our innermost being is for union with our true nature, our God-self, the Beloved.

Peace with our existence is what we yearn for but will never find by constantly trying to fulfill the myth of outer perfection. When we come into communion with the Self, then all the outer joys of the world are seen and appreciated with a whole new attitude. The time for such an awakening is now. And the place for awakening is you, right on the ground where you now stand.

Does this mean you will be a perfect human being in the eyes of the world? Probably not. The truth is you don't need to be perfect to reveal your inner treasures. You only need to be true to your Self and know that you are indeed all right already.

### Affirmation

*Today I make room in my heart for myself. My self-respect is reflected in my thoughts and actions. I respect the world in which all sentient beings and I live. I embrace my imperfect perfection and express a sense of humor even as I do my inner transformative work. Life is good, and I realize the preciousness of my human incarnation and that I am all right already.*

### Embodiment

From this space of connectivity, this space of fully participating in the nowness of this pure moment, I enter into the realm of ever-expanding good that some call heaven—the realm of infinite possibility, the realm of now. I am so connected to it that there is no battle between my inner life and my outer life. I now know, realize, accept, feel, that I am in heaven already.

I shift in this moment, knowing that regardless of how wonderful my life is, I'm barely scratching the surface of that which is within me. I am willing in this instant to set myself free.

I speak this word from my perfect imperfection. I know that my life is the life of beauty, and of love, and of intelligence, and of abundance, and of order and harmony. I am convinced that my life is the life of God and that this life, this eternal, timeless life is moving through me now. It now dissolves any coagulated thought forms that block, hinder, delay, or obstruct divine, compelling right action from taking place in my life.

My sense of self-acceptance does not come from the outer world. People, places, and things do not define who and what I really am. I define myself by acts of lovingkindness, compassion, generosity of heart, selfless service. Accepting all the goodness the universe has to offer me, I seek to do my part to share my resources with others. As I offer my skills, talents, and gifts to the world, I am humbled that they are accepted and appreciated. This encourages me to give even more. I know that my spiritual self-esteem is based on this expression.

I accept that I have a loving heart, an intelligent mind, an awakened Buddha nature within myself. I appreciate my outer expression of my inner self. I realize that I am a candidate for awakening, and I welcome into my life all that is required for this purpose. My prayer is that all beings awaken to their Authentic Self and gain spiritual merit from selfless actions.

## NOTES

1. Aurobindo Ghose, *The Life Divine* (Twin Lakes, Wisc.: Lotus Light Publications, 1949).
2. Ibid.
3. Osho, *Love, Freedom, and Aloneness: A New Vision of Relating* (New York: St. Martin's Press, 2001).
4. Lao-tzu, *Tao Te Ching*, trans. Stephen Mitchell (New York: Harper & Row, 1988).

# 13
# How to Prevent Identity Theft

*Something happened inside of me*
*I stepped into my true identity*
*I stopped and the Spirit got a hold of me*
*Something turned me 'round!*

Recently, my name and address were stolen from the ether of the internet and postal forms were submitted that rerouted my mail to Kenya. To my relief, everything was resolved without dire repercussions. An upside to the whole thing: it reminded me that there's nothing like direct, personal experience to open the heart to compassion.

We unquestionably consider identity to be our sole property. We alone have proprietorship to being a singular some-*one.* Thieves are not welcome in what is legally and personally private domain—especially the intimate territory of identity. Unfortunately, with technology's helping hand, identity theft can happen even when applying the most advanced precautions available.

Frank Abagnale, the world's most daring identity thief whose life story was the subject of the movie *Catch Me if You Can*, shares in the classes he teaches at the FBI Academy that all an identity thief needs today is a computer and within less than thirty minutes, all the information required to assume the identity of someone living or deceased is conveniently available.

My view is that whatever happens in my life is part of my spiritual practice. I suspect this is what caused me to make the leap from exploring the meaning of identity in general to contemplating these questions: What is the deeper meaning of identity—is it a solid or fluid thing? How do we identify ourselves with physical, mental, emotional, and spiritual accuracy? Who is the monolithic "me" that we describe in résumés, job interviews, online dating questionnaires, application forms, tax returns, and ultimately a death certificate? Does any of it come anywhere close to describing the reality that each of us is?

After I answered these questions for myself, I concluded that the most dangerous identify thief to be on the lookout for is *oneself.* If this surprises you, consider how your answers to the following questions apply to your relationship with your identity: How quickly do you give away your identity as an irreplaceably unique being and enter the game of social politics to fit in and be accepted by parents, a spouse, lovers, peers, clients, employers, a religious leader, organization, or social club? In what ways do the media and advertising influence you to compromise your life's vision, your appearance, your choice of friends, where you live, the car you drive, where you shop, what you eat? Does intimidation or fear of the opinions of others cause you to go against your own inner guidance? Does your religious affiliation teach that questioning its doctrines is sinful and against God's will?

This penetrating tidbit from Osho cuts through the whole issue: "The greatest fear is of losing one's identity, the image, the ego, the nameplate."[1] Is that why we purchase custom license plates and put bumper stickers on our cars that make public service announcements to other drivers about where we stand on subjects ranging from politics, abortion, spirituality, our favorite radio station, that our child was student of the month, to where we went on vacation? *Most of us invest tremendous energy in the identity we create, but to what degree is this investment, conscious or unconscious, grounded in wisdom or ignorance?*

Society exerts a powerful influence to create an identity that the outside world defines as successful, beautiful, hip, and so on. Most societal institutions are designed to assure that we are "properly socialized" from cradle to grave. We are so occupied measuring up to its standards, we hardly notice how we have been conditioned to give away our power, how we have been programmed to operate at a standard of mediocrity that doesn't support taking a stand for the changes we wish to see in the world.

## IDENTITY THEFT CHECKLIST

Countless times a day, individuals hold themselves hostage to the false beliefs they have about themselves, all the while demanding ransom from a world that is powerless to give what they are unwilling to give themselves: self-love, self-respect, and self-appreciation for their own spirit, beauty, wisdom, and creativity. *When you surrender your identity to the outer world, you become trapped in the dilemma of authentic self-expression versus superficial social expectation.* Do this long enough and an existential identity crisis occurs because you have stolen your identity and replaced it with a mask you wear to present yourself to the world. You may put a stop to this masquerade when you empower yourself to take self-responsibility for your life.

You are gracing the planet *now.* How do you want to live this precious human incarnation that has been given to you? As you explore your responses to the following identity theft checklist, practice honest self-observation without judging your findings:

How often do you withhold your authentic feelings or opinions to keep the peace, to not rock the boat?

When you interact with others, do you play small so that others may feel better about themselves? Or do you exaggerate your virtues to appear superior to others?

Do you try on different personas to determine which would be the most impressive and convincing under certain circumstances and in specific environments?

Do you continue to live under a belief system that no longer serves you so that other family members or friends won't get upset?

Do you automatically accept others' assessments of your identity without examining whether or not they vibe with your own inner sense of who you are?

## TWO CASES OF MISTAKEN IDENTITY

There are three ways of being in the world that offer clues about your relationship with your identity. First, there is task-oriented living wherein the fulfillment of life's responsibilities, obligations, and duties defines who you are. This offers safety and survival in a seemingly uncertain, unsafe world. At this stage, you also believe that what you do to earn a living is the central component of your being. Your profession is such an overriding aspect of your identity that when meeting a person you say your name followed by your job title. Likewise, when someone is introduced to you, you ask, "So, Miriam, what do you do?" Such individuals live in what I call the realm of "business-card consciousness."

Perhaps you believe that it is your duty to have the same profession as one of your parents, or to become a parent, or to make sure that your parents' desire to be grandparents is fulfilled, so you see your identity as being a dutiful son, daughter, and parent. Stepping out of the box is reckless, irresponsible, and scary to you, so the only safe choice is to perpetuate these familial expectations.

Such convictions cause a person to live in ways that are not much different from their forefathers. They may also live vicariously through others, impersonating or imitating their heroes and heroines, characters in movies and other fantasies, all the while suppressing and repressing their inner impulsion to grow, expand, and break out of the limited, mistaken identity they're stuck in.

Many individuals do not develop beyond task-oriented living because they are genuinely convinced that their identity is "What I do is who I am." They remain in a tight cocoon of agreement with this false notion, seldom breaking through it unless a major event shakes them at their roots. They are their own victims of mistaken identity, participating in what Alan Watts described as "the taboo against knowing who we are."

In addition to societal expectations and parental fantasies, identity is also forged by trendsetting celebrities, the media, educational and religious institutions—the list goes on. Individuality is sacrificed for the security of uniformity and acceptance, even the security of guaranteed rewards in the afterlife.

If it's painful for you to have read these descriptions, then consider yourself ready to begin reclaiming dominion over your life and moving closer to discovering the identity of your Authentic Self. Know, however, that this comes at a cost, one that you would eagerly pay if you could but see the luminosity of your Essential

Self, the exquisiteness that awaits your consent to express as the You of you. You must invest the spiritual coin of unbending intent to do the inner work required to reacquaint yourself with your-Self. It's like contemplating the Buddhist koan, "Show me the face you had before your parents were born."

The next way of navigating in the world is goal-oriented living. At this stage individuals exercise a certain amount of free choice about how and where they will invest their time and energies. They set their goals according to a combination of society's values and perhaps what they've read in books about what constitutes success. Independent thinking and risktaking are involved, along with consideration for the meaning of existence. This is especially the case when faced with such painful losses as divorce, the death of a loved one, getting laid off, or ailing health. A certain willingness to break self-imposed boundaries is motivated primarily by the zeal to accomplish one's list of goals, which provides a false sense of control over the outside world.

Goal-oriented individuals experience an occasional inner impulsion to more genuinely self-express, but they quickly repress or don't examine it too closely because of the fear it arouses in them. Their lives might get shaken up and become unpredictable; they may have to change, and the people who love them now may be left behind, or even worse, may leave them. Not to mention that they may have to revise or shorten their list of goals. These "doers" are most comfortable moving in a world of busyness dictated by long, detailed lists of things to do with great speediness. Aloneness for them is synonymous with loneliness, which they avoid at all costs. In truth, they are avoiding themselves by filling their calendars to keep the edge off as they confuse their goals with their purpose in life. While these individuals have moved from the survival mode to the useful mode, they remain convinced that their identity is "I am what I accomplish," which in the end is still just another case of mistaken identity.

## IMMUNITY AGAINST IDENTITY THEFT

The third way of being in the world is purpose-oriented living, where an individual consciously seeks and discovers answers to the perennial questions, "Who am I, and why am I here?" Such individuals are in the process of evolving from the useful mode into the creative mode of being. They continue to perform their tasks, fulfill their responsibilities, and set goals. The difference is that all of this unfolds in a spacious inner context of joy, creativity, and conscious communion with Spirit. Purpose-oriented individuals invite the spiritual qualities of love, compassion, peace, creativity, generosity of heart to express in, as, and through their lives. There's a celebration going on within them because their identity is rooted in the realization that "I am a unique expression of Spirit, living my life attuned to the evolutionary impulse governing the universe. My consciousness is open to infinite possibilities." This is the inner attitude that provides immunity against identity theft.

## YOUR TRUE IDENTITY IS IMMUNE TO THEFT

Ultimately, of course, no person, place, or circumstance can steal another's identity, nor can we steal our own. Even when we leave the body temple at the time of physical death, we participate in the continuum of existence. However, until we realize what constitutes the Essential Self—our core identity—we know we are alive but we are not yet living our fullest potential. *Discovering our true identity does not come about by merely learning feel-good spiritual descriptions about who we are but in unlearning the false conditioning by which we define and express our identity*. In other words, we must transform our patterns of thought and behavior.

**WHAT'S IN A NAME?**

I've observed with amusement that as some individuals become more self-acquainted with their unique characteristics, they want a name change to reflect their expanded perception of themselves. So they choose a new name, most often in a language other than English, which expresses a quality they have identified within themselves or are striving to cultivate. Upon learning more about their ancestry, individuals may be inspired to take a name that reflects an aspect of their personal history.

Sometimes a nickname comes closer to expressing a unique personality trait than a birth name, and so it sticks throughout a person's life. Today, more women choose to maintain their own surname when they marry, and married couples hyphenate their last names. And it's no longer so common for parental power to express by naming a son "Jr.", thus allowing him his own sense of individuality. Names do carry a vibration, which is why when monastics take vows they are given a new name that carries the energy of a spiritual quality or is associated with a saintly person. All of this relates to our intricate dance with identity.

Obviously, we don't get to choose our own names at birth, and carrying a name can be a vulnerable experience, as anyone who has been teased because of their name will attest. As a youngster, I never used or mentioned my middle name because it sounded old-fashioned. It was not so many years ago that I began using my middle name out of great respect for my namesake, my grandfather, Francis Bernard, and my father, who was named after his father, both of whom are a tremendous inspiration in my life. Not long ago I felt that I had matured into my middle name and now use it consistently.

Nonfiction and fiction books that forecast future societal trends make reference to a time when individuals will no longer be identified by a name. Instead, they will be given a number. Talk about an in-your-face insult to identity! Our true identity will always be more than a number, our gender, or name because we are, in essence, formless and nameless. Our spirit-soul knows only its cosmic identity as an individualized emanation of our Source. Nevertheless, for the sake of having some fun playing with your name as an aspect of your identity, if you could rename yourself today, what might your name be? If you could rename your children, what might their names be? Upon what would you base your choices?

## IDENTIFY YOURSELF WITH FIRST CAUSE

As stated earlier, your cosmic identity is made in the image and likeness of love, intelligence, compassion, joy, creativity, and beauty itself. It includes the unique ways in which these qualities express in, through, and as you. Embody this realization, and you will cease competing for love, recognition, and attention. You will know that you are one of a kind, that your life is on purpose, and that you are loved, guarded, and guided by Existence. When you say "yes" to authentically being who you are, your purpose reveals itself in language your heart can understand. Then, instead of operating from cunningness and manipulating the world around you, you navigate life from your identification with First Cause, your Source.

As you begin to touch who and what you really are, you participate in the art of real living. From the boardroom to the meditation room to the bathroom sink, the impress of the uniqueness of your being energetically falls upon all that encompasses your world.

A trustworthy and accurate indicator that you are moving toward reclaiming your true identity is when your life centers on your inner evolution. You begin your search for a spiritual path that makes sense to your heart and your head, one that teaches you how to expand consciousness and become a beneficial presence on the planet. You affirmatively answer the call to deliver your talents, gifts, and skills with nonattachment to the fruits of your actions. You live free from the shackles of societal thought forms that would bind you into a collective agreement with the status quo. You begin to attain self-mastery over your thought patterns, your behavior patterns. You accept the invitation of the master teacher Jesus to "come out from among them" and dare to be your Authentic Self.[2]

When you realize that you are on the planet as a co-creative agent to fully express your unique identity, you are claiming that you are a distribution center for delivering what is happening throughout the cosmos: love, beauty, compassion, joy, creativity, harmony, peace. Challenges arise, but you relate to them in their proper context—as rich material to work with.

As you begin to love and appreciate yourself, you realize that all beings are an emanation of First Cause, and so it becomes natural to express compassion and forgiveness and pray for everyone to experience the glory of their existence. *You begin to realize that how you see the world and what you experience are projections from your own consciousness. Equipped with this insight, you quit demanding that circumstances and people change, and instead you take self-responsibility and work within yourself for a transformation in consciousness.* You consciously choose to live by the evolutionary principles governing the universe. You accept that there is an innate greatness within you which must be disturbed into action, so you welcome challenges as a vehicle for awakening to your true nature. You begin each day with an attitude that "this is the best day of my life, and by the end of this day, I will have a deeper realization about the universe, about the Invisible, about myself and the true art of living." In these ways, you go about living the wisdom that your true identity is not determined by anything or anyone outside of yourself.

Existence is whispering in your ear right now that everything you could ever hope to be is already who you are. Believe it. What does that feel like? How does it affect your thoughts, choices, and actions?

Right now, through meditation, contemplation, visioning, and affirmative prayer, you can begin to see your original face, feel your innately enlightened state, and be on your way to freedom from the illusion of an existence separate from the Whole. You will know yourself as an expression of the next level of human evolution, and never again will you have the need to compromise your real identity.

### Affirmation

*I give my consent to activating my life's purpose of delivering my talents, gifts, and skills on the planet—not only for my personal benefit, but as my contribution to the planet. Anything that heretofore blocked or intimidated me from living up to my highest potential mentally, emotionally, creatively, or spiritually is now dissolved. I am who and what I was always meant to be.*

### Embodiment

Right here and right now, I announce the truth that my life is the life of God. I fully accept my spiritual inheritance of the qualities of the Spirit and activate them within me. Pure love, intelligence, wisdom, and beauty emanate from my soul. Everything works together for my good. The entire universe is conspiring on its own behalf to release life energy through me in all aspects of my life.

All the ways in which I was previously tied to my human identity that would have convinced me I am separate from the Whole are now dissolved. They were never the truth about who and what I am. I am beyond my personal history, beyond my ego, beyond the ego's opinions, concepts, and points of view. I no longer see myself only with the mortal eye but with the inner eye of the Spirit. In its reflection I see my inherent purity, my innately awakened state.

I not only see who and what I really am, I act from this place of awareness. From the mundane to the sublime, I infiltrate all of my thoughts and actions with the qualities of my true nature. My life is the life of God; God's life is my life. I am what Thou art; Thou art what I am. In this realization I know all of my needs are met. I know I am an opening, an instrumentality through which the Eternal shines forth and expresses through. This is my true identity, and I wear it well.

This word that I have spoken falls upon a fertile consciousness. I declare my readiness to live that which I believe. The conditions are now ripe within me to be fully franchised expression of the dynamic potential, vitality, and vigor that I am.

I no longer fall prey to identity theft, to the false belief that I am separate from the Whole of Existence. I serve this truth today in my thoughts, speech, and actions and am filled with the joy of not only knowing but of *being* who and what I truly am.

## Notes

1. Osho, *Courage: The Joy of Living Dangerously* (New York: St. Martin's Press, Griffin, 1991).
2. 2 Corinthians 6:17.

# 14
# Spiritually Liberating Livelihood

*A life of service is now my mission*
*And all that I pray for is already given*

Business is evolving a more enlightened view that considers clients as individuals one has the privilege of serving and with whom meaningful relationships can be cultivated. The delivery of a product or service is a way through which we serve and connect to one another. Circulating the energy called money is our form of exchange.

During the services at Agape, a collection is taken. I teach that money is an energy-promissory note to be delivered at a later date. In other words, we don't bless money, we bless the energy that will be freed by the money as it takes the form of staff, philanthropic projects, donations to other organizations doing good in the world—you get the idea. When we consider money as only that which allows us to be consummate consumers instead of the creativity and beauty that it can manifest, money can become destructive. The more prosperous and generous we become, the more we honor the promise in promissory.

Those who go into business simply for money have yet to realize how business for profit alone has caused tremendous damage to our planet and its people. Such individuals are behind the times and have not yet realized that today people seek to align their personal values with their livelihood and purchases. When you work just for profit, this is an unevolved approach to livelihood. Noble profit is defined as that which is used not only to support our livelihood but to help create a kind and just society.

## SPIRITUALIZING LIVELIHOOD

Spiritualizing business begins with "spirit," which comes from the Latin word *spiritus* and means *breath.* It is Spirit that breathes the creative life force into all expressions of existence, including business. The convergence of science and spirituality fosters the realization that we live, move, and have our being in a unified field of energy that interconnects all life, including the web of commerce. The lines drawn between the corporate and nonprofit sectors are becoming blurred. Those in the business world increasingly realize that we are a cross-cultural people with a capacity to organize for the shared purpose of improving life on the planet. There is a growing awareness that the impact of products and services upon people returns to a business and its leadership as the energy that they put out into the world. William W. George, Professor of Management Practices at Harvard Business School, expresses it this way: "We are all spiritual beings. To unleash the whole capability of the individual—mind, body and spirit—gives enormous power to the organization. This has nothing to do with religion. People of many faiths, or no faith at all for that matter, can join together in a common cause of service to others through their work."[1]

Remarkable things are emerging from this evolutionary approach to business. Walk into any Target store today and you will see a large display describing the humanitarian programs to which it contributes $3 million per week, 5 percent of pretax profits, to education, the arts, and social services. Tom Chappell, CEO of Tom's of Maine, famous for its toothpastes and soaps, donates 10 percent of his pretax profits to philanthropic causes and gives his employees four paid hours a month to volunteer for community service.

When interviewed about his products ranging from salad dressings and popcorn to dog food, Paul Newman indicated that he and his wife, actress Joanne Woodward, first went to Hollywood seeking to become actors who were well compensated for their art. While they were successful in reaching these goals, something still felt missing in their lives until they realized that they wanted to give back to the world in a meaningful way. Since 1982, they have given $200 million to thousands of charities worldwide through Newman's Own Organics. They were forerunners—along with individuals like Dr. David Bronner and his soaps, and Ben and Jerry's Ice Cream—in changing the face of how we do business and how people purchase with more than savings in mind. Think about this: We each become philanthropists simply by purchasing products from companies whose profits benefit humanity. While money for shareholders remains a business responsibility, today companies are increasing their respect for their employees and the larger community, thus meeting this goal at a reduced expense to the environment, human rights, public safety, and health.

## CONSCIOUSNESS BIRTHS CONSCIENCE

Spirituality and profitability are not mutually exclusive. Go into any bookstore and you will find shelves filled with books reflecting the emerging trend of introducing spiritual principles in the workplace. Look online or in magazines and you will see ads devoted to conferences that promote enlightened leadership and business practices. *Leadership* is an Old English word that means "to go first," which underscores how the consciousness of an organization's leadership has a major impact on a business, its employees, and the world at large. *Whether led by an individual or a team, organizational structure cannot evolve collectively without its leadership first experiencing a transformation of consciousness.*

Prayer and meditation are no longer uncommon in business environments. Apple Computer's offices have a meditation room and staff is given half an hour a day to meditate and pray. My publisher, Beyond Words, encourages body, mind, spirit living by offering personal-development courses, stocking healthy, organic snacks in their lunchroom, and giving weekly back and foot massages. I was delighted to learn that Sounds True, an audio/video production company in Colorado, has a meditation room and offers meditation classes to its staff. Rhino Records in Los Angeles provides healthy in-house meals and massages for its employees. Other company offerings include yoga, deep breathing, tai chi, and other stress reduction practices. At the Agape International Spiritual Center, the organization I founded, we stop each day from 3:00 PM to 3:30 PM to meditate, and we have prayer partners who offer affirmative prayer support. Once a month, the entire Agape community of ten-thousand local members is invited to participate in a Visioning session to co-create the ever-evolving vision and mission of the Agape Movement.

All of these organizations—and I have named only a few—offer empirical evidence that consciousness births a conscience that seeks to be a beneficial presence on the planet. This includes minimizing our ecological footprint, vital to future generations.

Whole Foods market co-president Walter Robb expresses a beautiful approach: "We're not retailers who have a mission—we're missionaries who retail."

### FROM DARWIN'S SURVIVING TO CULTURAL THRIVING

The purpose of business is threefold: the fulfillment of society's living needs and the creation of an environment in which happiness and self-development may flourish and art and beauty are encouraged. All else is an invasion of the ego into business endeavors.

Long ago, our life was based on a model of survival that bred a sense of competition between tribes, villages, businesses, and nations. Darwinian theory taught survival of the fittest based on a belief in scarcity, so the fittest individuals were the ones who got the goods. This model is extinct because we actually live in a world of plentitude. Those who build relationships, cooperate, and collaborate—not those who overpower—not only survive, they thrive.

Businesses and leadership that focus on scarcity and competition cause harm to themselves, their communities, their clients, and humanity. They do not evolve. While a successful business model must be based on sound business practices, service combined with the principle of oneness, the interconnectedness of all life, forms an enlightened point of view with long-term benefits. The species that experiences the highest level of cooperation and collaboration also possesses the strongest tendencies to thrive and evolve, which is an outer demonstration of the inner power of intent.

### ENLIGHTENED BUSINESS SUPPORTS THE WEB OF LIFE.

*BusinessWeek* reported that 95 percent of Americans no longer support the notion that a corporation's only purpose is the greedy bottom line. There have been major backlashes over the CEOs in powerful corporations who have profited billions of dollars while causing individuals to lose their jobs and homes because of corporate mismanagement and greed. In the consciousness of the mature individual, money is the by-product of walking in the direction of our life's purpose. Such individuals do not consider their livelihood as simply a resource for hard, cold cash but as an avenue for their creativity, for the sharing of their gifts, talents, passions, and resources.

When one's product or service is delivered from a platform of creativity, generosity, service, excellence, integrity, and beauty, then the whole web of life is uplifted. People will beat a path to the door of such a business. There may be many other businesses in the marketplace selling the same product or offering the same services, but people are willing to pay more when they feel the energy of creativity and service—they pay more because they know they are receiving more.

From a progressive point of view, once career success has been achieved, it's time to support the web of life by applying the principles that helped you become personally successful to creating global success so that every man, woman, boy, and girl may have their needs met. To keep on making money for its own sake is to remain stuck in an inner world that is selfish and claustrophobic. It's time to play a bigger game, to make a bigger contribution to the planet than personal success only, which is just one aspect in your overall development. *The point is to create a system where individuals don't work simply for money or personal gain but to support the planet and its inhabitants in entering the next stage of evolutionary progression.* This equals an expansion of mutuality, collaboration, cooperation, compassion, peace, and prosperity for all.

## THE PRACTICE AND POWER OF VISIONING

In 1986, when I founded the Agape International Spiritual Center, I did so applying a process I was developing at the time and have since trademarked as the Life Visioning Process. This process is equally effective in professional environments as it is in one's personal life.

Spiritual integrity is a tangible energy that greatly impacts an organization. It is an agent of progress in an organization that taps into what wants to emerge as the next level of human expression. As much as we'd like to place spiritual organizations and houses of worship in a separate category, they also are businesses in that they must support themselves monetarily—everything that you'd expect from any business. There is no inconsistency with spirituality and the business of raising the money it takes to finance a spiritual organization. It's a matter of how this goal is achieved that is important. So beginning with a small group who shared my vision, we entered the inner laboratory of the Life Visioning Process to receive input from the universe as to how we were to build a trans-denominational spiritual center of diverse, like-minded individuals.

We began by placing questions, one at a time, before Divine Intelligence. We asked, "What is Spirits' vision of our spiritual community?" We then entered silence and through meditation became open and receptive to intuitive guidance. Afterwards, each person in the circle shared their insights. (This is a very over-simplified description of the fundamental step in the visioning process for the purpose of providing you a glimpse into how it works.)

## KEYS FOR PROFESSIONAL AND PERSONAL SUCCESS

The growing recognition of the interconnectedness of body, mind, and spirit is excellent news for our society because it acknowledges that success in any endeavor begins with an integral approach. Ignoring any of aspects of being causes a gap in one's ability to function harmoniously. As part of the staff training at Agape, we teach seven keys that allow each individual to experience a flourishing personal and professional life.

We begin by emphasizing the importance of cultivating a healthy body temple, which in turn supplies the vibrant energy required for the body's cells to replicate themselves so that individuals may function at their creative peak. When we are healthy, we have a greater chance of being conduits for what is seeking to emerge at this particular stage of our planet's evolution.

So the first key is to have adequate hydration provided by clean, pure water. There is a metaphysical aspect to hydration mentioned in the Bible when Jesus is at the well with a Samaritan woman: "Whoever drinks of the water that I shall give him will become in him a fountain of water springing up into everlasting life."[2] In this statement, Jesus indicated that he was teaching a way of life based on the living water of spiritual realization. Today's application of his words may be interpreted to mean that by living a life based on spiritual principles one will not thirst for get-rich-quick schemes or popular trends that offer external happiness only, that by drinking from the font of inner wisdom the soul's thirst will be quenched.

The second key is good nutrition. On the physical level, this has to do with eating live foods that carry life force and the light of the natural world. Nourishing your body with something that's been touched by sunlight, something fresh that your body can assimilate into energy, supports your immune system and maintains health.

In the metaphysical sense, nourishment also refers to the quality of conversations you have, such as when Jesus said, "Hear me everyone, and understand: There is nothing that enters a man from the outside which can defile him; but the things which come out of him, those are the things that defile a man."[3] This refers not only to what you eat but also to the conversations that you have, the types of books you read, the movies you see, the people you hang out with, because as you internalize their influences, their impress in your consciousness becomes the tenor of your outer expressions, "the things which come out of you."

The third key is exercise. In order for your body to fully assimilate vitamins, minerals, food, and water, you must move your body. Without exercise, there's little assimilation, and proper elimination cannot take place. This is why many businesses now have gyms, yoga practice, tai chi, and other forms of circulating energy throughout the body for maintaining a level of vitality and stimulation that may be applied to creativity, artistry. Metaphysically, inner exercise occurs when we are faithful to our spiritual practices, when we practice what we profess to believe.

To agree with the keys described here is one thing, to practice them is another. To read and study and have conversations about spiritual principles is good, but unless you incorporate them into your life, you won't embody or integrate them—which means you aren't receiving their benefits. Ask yourself, "How can I now move from theory into practice?" *If you merely collect spiritual information without practicing it, all you will develop is a case of spiritual indigestion and constipation.* There is no substitute for practice. Trust, then practice. Even if at first you don't feel trust, practice anyway and the results will reveal that the universe is trustworthy.

The fourth key is detoxification. In the physical sense, this means fasting for the purpose of releasing toxins stored in the skin as well as all of the other organs of elimination. If your current state of health permits, it is good to drink only liquids or eat less than you normally do at least one day of the week so that the body has an opportunity to cleanse itself and the digestive system is given a rest. You may want to do some research, and of course speak to your healthcare provider or nutritionist to learn what kind of fasting or cleansing program would work best for your body type and health history.

On the spiritual plane, we must also practice forgiveness to purify our hearts and minds. Accumulated feelings of anger, resentment, and hurt become toxic in the body. These emotions have to go somewhere, especially if they are repressed or suppressed. What they do is become lodged in the body temple. Individuals sometimes hesitate to forgive—both themselves and others—because they think that this lets themselves or others off the hook of accountability, but each person stands responsible for their behaviors. Therefore, we needn't set up ourselves as their final arbiter. Let us instead take responsibility for cleaning our inner household of negative emotions. Forgiveness is often what the heart is waiting for in order to release the past and be in the now.

The fifth key is giving consent to the reality that we live in a friendly, trustworthy, supportive universe. In the physical and mental sense, in order for the body to stay vibrant and strong, it is vital to wake up every single day sensing and knowing that you are mothered by the universe. Life is on your side, cheering you on. If you have toxic thoughts that the universe is unfriendly, that it's chaotic and out to get you, then you are giving yourself the message that you are unsafe, that life is unsafe, that you may become a victim of the unknown. Doubt, fear, worry, and anxiety then rule your awareness and produce toxic chemicals rather than tonic chemicals and undermine your nervous and immune systems. This creates the conditions for disease.

When you realize that you may trust the fundamental goodness of the universe, it also means that you believe in possibilities—and infinite are the possibilities. In the summer of 1998, when the Agape International Spiritual Center was moving from one location to another, we had to renovate our new facility before we could occupy it. This meant both paying our new monthly lease and paying the hotel where we were renting their largest meeting room for our Wednesday and Sunday services, while continuing to pay construction costs and staff salaries. My board of trustees and I were pressed against the financial ropes.

Some board members felt that we lacked both the money and the time to meet the city's inspection deadlines in order to open by the time of our twelfth anniversary in November. It was a perfect situation in which to practice our conviction that Agape had a vision and mission that was divinely inspired and supported and that the funds to continue construction and paying salaries would be provided. There were times when we felt we were finding a way out of seemingly no way, that we were affirming the impossible.

During a pivotal board meeting, I asked each of the eight members to give their unconditional consent to knowing that we would open the doors to our new sanctuary by our twelfth anniversary. "I'm not asking you if we can do this," I explained, "I'm asking you if it is possible that it be done, that we can stay in the realm of such a possibility. We don't have to know how—just if it's possible." Apparently this was more challenging for them than I had anticipated, so to make the point, I got up and locked the office door, adding, "None of us are leaving this office until we sense that anything is possible." We arrived at a consensus—it was a possibility. Our contractor, not an Agape member, was also in the meeting, pensively absorbing the contents of our entire conversation. We'd had two flyers printed—one saying we were going to discontinue our services at the hotel and close our doors until the construction was completed, and a second one announcing the opening of our new building in November. We agreed to send out the second flyer.

Two days flew by and still there was no indication that we would raise enough money to complete the construction in order to open our sanctuary doors. We had already applied for a loan from a bank in our community with whom we didn't have a working relationship. On the third day, we received a call from the bank. It seemed that the bank president noticed a loan officer reviewing a file and inquired about what he was studying so intensely. When he learned that Agape was applying for this loan he said, "Beckwith? Give it to him." I did not know this man personally. Next, our building contractor said he was so moved during our earlier board meeting that he announced that he was going to double his construction crew and complete the work without pay in time for the city inspector to sign off on the job. We opened in November, albeit to cement floors and no air conditioning in ninety degree weather.

Imagine our joy when thousands gathered to celebrate the inauguration of our new facility. From that day onward, when challenges arise—as they do in any organization—we refer back to those days when our unwavering reliance on the fundamental goodness of the universe gave us the strength to accept that all things are possible.

The sixth key is light. In the physical sense, you need a proper dosage of sunlight everyday. The sun itself is not harmful because the universe has not been created chaotically. We need a certain amount of natural sunlight of at least 20 minutes a day so that we may absorb the sun's healing qualities for the production of vitamin D as well as other vitamins and chemicals. Each of us has to apply common sense in finding the balance for our own body type.

"Quantum" is a discreet quantity of electromagnetic energy, a burst of light that goes on and off. The universe is made up of bursts of quantum that give the appearance that things are solid, or continual. Between our body cells there is luminosity, quantum energy. Although we appear to be solid entities, we are in fact made up of light energy, the stuff of cosmic creation. Nothing is as solid as it appears to the five senses; everything that exists is simply vibrating at different rates of light-energy. Interiorizing practices such as meditation allow us to begin to inwardly see with the light of the soul that we are more than the body, that we are luminous beings.

The seventh key is rest. We must find time for deep inner rest so that our body cells and mental and emotional nervous systems may regenerate. What this means is making time for no-thought, coming to a complete stop, being still, and realizing the wisdom that engaging in nonaction is a vital form of action. This seventh key completes the template for experiencing the organic Wholeness that exists within.

The livelihood in which we engage to support our lives and the spiritual practices we incorporate into our daily routine are for the same purpose: to experience the flourishing life we are meant to live. The universe does not recognize the human tendency to compartmentalize life. So whether it's in our livelihood or the intimate details of our life, the laws of authentic success are equally operative. It is to our professional and personal advantage to access these laws and practice them. Then, as sure as the day follows the night, we will reap authentic success that comes from sharing our gifts, talents, skills, and resources. We will be counted among those who possess a heart of generosity and compassion that is as wide as the world.

### Affirmation

*I acknowledge my desire to realize personal and professional success. I fully express my gifts, talents, and skills. I know that through my spirit of generosity, by holding back nothing, the universe fully supports me and sources my good in like measure. I give thanks for this co-creative, reciprocal relationship and enter into it with trust, integrity, and commitment.*

### Embodiment

I acknowledge the web of interconnectedness within all aspects of my life. There is no separation between my personal and professional life. Whether I am employed or retired, my gifts, talents, skills and consciousness continue to express and impact my world.

I live in alignment with the physical laws governing the body of the universe and know that they are replicated in my own physical body. With respectful attention, I hydrate my body with clean, pure water. I imbibe it and know that it stimulates my brain power, supports my immune system, vitalizes my body, and cleanses my organs. In meditation, I drink of the living waters that freely flow throughout my inner spirit.

I give thanks for the light of the universe that births and supports the food, vitamins, and minerals that nourish my body temple. I acknowledge my understanding that it is not only the food that I take in that supports my existence but the very life force that provides the intelligence to digest, assimilate, and eliminate it. I cooperate with the laws governing the maintenance of a strong body, a creative mind. I ingest wholesome ideas and inspiration from my relationships with others and am grateful to my friends through whom Love itself blesses me.

I actively practice forgiveness as an act of conscious detoxification of my physical, mental, and emotional bodies. I realize that as I do so my mind becomes vitalized to create, to offer my skills in the workplace. I make it a daily practice to forgive those who have knowingly or unknowingly hurt me in any way, and I inwardly ask the forgiveness of anyone I have knowingly or unknowingly hurt. My inner household is now cleansed of any residue of toxins.

How good it is to know that I live in a friendly, supportive universe of infinite possibility. I merge my consciousness in its light of love, intelligence, and order. I offer my gifts to the planet not for personal recognition but because I want to make a positive contribution to my world and to all beings. I live up to my highest knowledge of all that this means, and I consciously choose to evolve my awareness of the laws of the universe. I practice what I learn, what I believe to be true, and give thanks for my capacity to do so.

## Notes

1. W. George William, quoted in *The New Bottom Line,* ed. John Renesch (San Francisco: New Leader's Press, 1995).
2. John 4:14.
3. Mark 7:1.

# 15
# Minding Your Spiritual Manners on Planet Earth

*When your feet are placed on higher ground*
*You can hear the holy sound, you can feel God's*
*presence all around in the holy sound of*
*Om, peace, shanti, shalom*

As a spiritual being having a human incarnation, you are a beloved guest on planet Earth. Your consummate host, Spirit, has put on a display of cosmic beauty as the backdrop for your journey. You have been equipped for your Earth pilgrimage with all the love, wisdom, joy, peace, compassion, generosity, and creativity to make your adventure enlightening and entertaining. With so much unconditional love, support, and grace at your disposal, are you minding your spiritual manners?

As we go through a typical day, most of us rely on the etiquette training we received earlier in life to make a favorable impression in our interactions with others. The word *etiquette* was coined by the gardener of King Louis XIV. The original meaning of the French *etiquets* was literally, "keep off the grass," and though its meaning changed over the centuries, its intent remained the same: to create mindfulness-based interactions with other individuals and one's world. Manners are a system of respect. A modern day expert on etiquette, Emily Post, offers us a view of twentieth-century manners beyond the dining-room table: "Manners are a sensitive awareness of the feelings of others. If you have that awareness, you have good manners, no matter what fork you use."

Some consider manners artificial, an invasion of personal freedom, or simply passé, but in truth they are energy-actions that carry a vibration which becomes a personal advertisement about who we are and what we value.

Pier M. Forni, a professor at Johns Hopkins University and author of *Choosing Civility: The Twenty-five Rules of Considerate Conduct*, supports Ms. Post's view, saying, "I am absolutely convinced—and branches of quantum physics back this up—that everything, including our thoughts, choices, behaviors, and actions, are energy and have a beneficial or harmful impact, depending upon what the individual puts forth in every moment of every day."[1]

## YOUR EARTH WALK: A REVELATION OF SPIRIT'S IMPECCABLE ETIQUETTE

Your name is on the A-list for a cosmic happening: an invitation to realize total aliveness, a state of being that Matthew Fox called "radical amazement." Another way of putting it is that as a cherished guest of our Source, the entire banquet of life has been spread out before us to taste-test its rich ingredients. The plate of your life may be filled with all sorts of appetizers, entrées, and desserts, some which you will consider delicious and others that you will want to spit out the minute they enter your experience.

Oddly, many individuals do not have a mental, emotional, and spiritual diet that offers genuine nourishment. It takes some experimenting, some sampling of life-choices. Of all the species on the planet, the human being alone has an inherent taste for enlightenment and the ability to realize it. It is this innate capacity to wake up that caused Buddhists to describe a human incarnation as very precious. That we have appeared on the stage of life with an innate longing to realize our true nature and equipped with all that is needed to do so is a reflection of Spirit's good faith relationship with us, its impeccable etiquette. It is up to us if we are going to fully accept and reciprocate this gesture of unconditional love. The Spirit is too humble to force itself upon us, to coerce us into a relationship of mutuality. Its joy comes from a freewill offering of our love, gratitude, and the full-out use of our gifts, talents, and skills.

### GRATITUDE: THE BIRTH OF SPIRITUAL MANNERS

Gratitude for existence is the first act of a gracious guest. It is an expression of our appreciation for life with all of its infinite possibilities. We have been given free choice, which places in our hands the key to exercising dominion over our life. We do not live by instinct; we have the power to exercise conscious choice and to learn and grow from the choices we make. How self-reliantly we have been designed! We are free to follow our dreams, to change our minds at any given moment and go in an entirely different direction. As we grow in appreciation for having been entrusted to co-create our destiny, we deepen our commitment to live up to our highest potential. *Gratitude is where freedom and the creation of our destiny meet.*

Are you grateful that your body operates in such a way that every day you don't have to learn all over again how to breathe, walk, talk, sleep, eat, or digest your food? These activities seem so basic to existence that it is easy to take them for granted. The more you study and learn about the body, its anatomy, chemistry, and biology, the more amazing, even miraculous, the body becomes. When we begin to relate to the body as a temple that houses the inner spirit, we begin to make new choices about how to care for it so that it may function at its optimum level. Science is only now catching up to what the mystics have always known and taught about the body-mind-spirit interconnection. Expand your knowledge of how the body, brain, mind, and spirit interact, and you will be awed by your power to consciously influence their functions. A new gratitude will enter your heart for the miracle that is You.

We begin to mind our spiritual manners on planet Earth when we give thanks for the gift of an incarnation that is perfectly designed to navigate the vast terrain of human existence.

**ENTHUSIASM: THE FUEL OF SPIRITUAL MANNERS**

Enthusiasm is from the Greek *entheos*, which means "God in us." What does it mean to say that God is "in" us? It means that we have inherited the qualities of our Source; they are part and parcel of our innate being. Who wouldn't be enthusiastic about having a birthright of unconditional love, bliss, compassion, intelligence, happiness, wisdom, joy, creativity, clarity, wholeness, opulence? Enthusiasm enables us to choose to go with the flow of life including all of its challenges, blessings, and open-ended opportunities with full confidence that each circumstance is intended to accelerate our evolution.

This very moment you may become enthusiastic about the infinite possibilities that lie before you, and especially those that lie within you. When we are enthusiastic we move with an affirmative energy that propels us to skillfully and joyously meet all that comes into our experience. We explore the life-lessons in our experiences, welcome them, and take them to heart. Enthusiasm is not something you have to create; it is an organic quality of your consciousness. You have only to invite it forth, to let it arise from within you and let it fuel your endeavors, your creative expressions, and your interactions with others. Enthusiasm will put the smile of the Buddha upon your face.

### INTEGRITY: THE BACKBONE OF SPIRITUAL MANNERS

Character is considered to be the sum total of our traits. However, character is not mere personality; it is behavior patterns formed by the evolution of our individual perceptions, beliefs, opinions, understanding, insights, values, and attitudes. When these operate in harmony with the laws of the universe, we live in fundamental integrity. We mind our spiritual manners by walking our talk, honoring our commitments, being true to our word. There is congruency in what we think, say, and do.

The Greek etymology of *character* means "to inscribe." In Middle English it is defined as a distinctive mark or imprint. So it would be accurate to say that character is the etching of God upon your innermost spirit. Integrity is not developed through will power or behavior modification; it is a revelation of our essential nature, which is made in the image and likeness of our Source. Integrity is not a religious or moral code; it is living by the universal spiritual principles that govern the universe. Integrity does not mean that we never error or fall short of our intentions but that we have the spiritual backbone to catch ourselves, make amends where necessary, and get back on track. It is trusting that in spite of our missteps, Spirit's integrity never changes and unconditional love, compassion, and forgiveness are continuously sent our way as encouragement for us to step back into our integrity. When we live in integrity, peace reigns in our inner world.

### RESPECT: THE HEART OF SPIRITUAL MANNERS

There is some confusion in our understanding of respect. It is not obligatory obedience to persons who are in positions of authority.

When expressed under forced conditions that are motivated by fear, respect is not genuine.

Respect is the recognition that all beings, all that exists, is sourced by the Infinite and therefore imbued with its Essence. When we consciously realize this, we treat ourselves, others, Mother Nature, even seemingly inanimate objects with respect. The Spirit's respect for its creation reverberates in every corner of the cosmos. It is a palpable energy that we can feel and emulate in our relationship with life.

It was the eighteenth-century German philosopher Immanuel Kant who put respect for oneself and others at the core of moral theory based on the conviction that every individual has an absolutely essential dignity. When we express respect to a person, it goes forth from us as a potent vibration which quickens that person's own self-respect. Neither diamonds, rubies, nor gold show honor as much as when we offer genuine respect from our hearts. No love-offering supercedes a genuine expression of respect.

Genuine respect prevents us from acts of hypocrisy. If our "respect" is motivated by fear, it is just that—fear, which, we may have been erringly taught, equals respect. Respect is one of the highest expressions of love. The art of respecting begins with self-respect, and self-respect generates respect for others. When genuine respects wells up in our hearts, even if we are not able to verbalize it to another person to our satisfaction, they will feel its vibration—respect is that powerful an energy.

### GENEROSITY: THE ACTIVITY OF SPIRITUAL MANNERS

One of my favorite expressions is that *we give to live, until we live to give.* As we realize that our spiritual inheritance includes the entire treasure house of Good, we acknowledge our gratitude for this through our spirit of generosity. We reciprocate the Spirit's lavish givingness by openly and frequently expressing generosity toward all life through the sharing of our resources, time, energy, gifts, talents, and skills.

Generosity is contagious and leaves a profound effect on both the giver and the receiver. As Jesus the Christ said, "As you give, so shall you receive."[2] The word *generous* comes from the Latin *genus*, which means "origin, source." Conscious, spontaneous giving is expressed through our thoughtfulness, lovingkindness, compassion, and sensitivity toward the needs of our brothers and sisters, animals—all life. May we all strive to be paragons of generosity!

When we are generous, we are compassionate. One of the highest forms of compassion is the understanding of a person's lack of understanding. *Sympathy asks, "How do you feel?" Empathy says, "I will feel for you." Compassion says, "I understand. How can I serve to alleviate your suffering?"* Generosity softens the hard places in our heart. As our heart opens, we experience a sense of expansion of prosperity in our time, energy, financial, and other resources.

Generosity is a currency of circulation. As we allow unlimited substance to flow through us, we discover that we have more to give and share because we have tapped directly into the divine storehouse. Our sense of having enough to spare and share comes from the gold mine hidden in our spirit, which causes us to joyously give of our tangible and intangible resources. Generosity is our simple but powerful manner of saying "thank you" to Existence.

### CREATIVITY: THE SOUL OF SPIRITUAL MANNERS

Creativity is the very pulse of our life. We cannot move, breathe, blink our eyes, or think without setting creative energy into motion. When we open to our innate creativity, we graciously acknowledge the Power behind all the powers that have been given to us.

Each of us expresses creativity in our own unique way, according to our originality of being. As we evolve into the more existential aspects of being, we tap into the sizzling juices of creativity. Everyone is consciously or unconsciously involved in the act of co-creating his or her life. The world is begging for creativity, not imitation. The more consciously we participate, the more we will be original, not an imitation of someone else. Each of us has a soul-mandate from Spirit to be creative, to not walk lockstep with mediocrity or business as usual. This means that we are meant to be progressive, innovative, inspiring, beautifying, all with practical benefits.

The greatest artistic achievement is how we live our life. We are meant to live on the creative edge of self-discovery and self-expression. When we don't live by this mandate we blaspheme the potential within us. Each of us is a co-creative being made in the image of the Ineffable, and the primordial field of infinite possibility is within us. Not to activate this potential violates your assignment to be You and prevents the evolutionary impulse from flowing through you.

In this world nothing remains stagnant. If we are not consciously co-creating, our creative muscles become atrophied. Be conscious of your creative anatomy. It will rejuvenate you and give you entry into your inner world so that you may vitalize your environment with its elixir of delight. Your creativity is the imprint you make on the canvas of your life and the lives of others. You are a vibrant life-artist who is fully capable of joyously minding your spiritual manners as you participate in creation's cosmic dance.

### Affirmation

*It is easy for me to mind my spiritual manners because I know who and what I am as an emissary of the Spirit on earth. I surrender to life in full awareness and gratitude for all the gifts that have been freely given by Existence. So with utmost respect for my individual life and that of all beings, creatures, and nature, I simply say thank you Infinite Spirit.*

### Embodiment

How grateful I am for my existence, for that of my loved ones, my community, my country, and my world. Beauty and bountifulness are everywhere present, reminders that I live in a world of opulence that advertises the Spirit's omnipresence. I walk in gratitude for all the blessings that are present in my life and especially for the capacity to love, to develop mindfulness and awareness.

I give thanks for my body temple, the miraculous way in which it functions. I do not take my health for granted and express self-respect by properly caring for my body, my mind, and my spirit. I acknowledge their interconnectedness and mindfully nourish these aspects of my being.

I enthusiastically approach my spiritual growth and development, including my challenges. The energy of enthusiasm gives me the power to persevere, to not give up on myself or others. My spiritual practices are infused with enthusiasm causing me to maintain a daily routine of meditation, affirmative prayer, introspection, and spiritual study.

My life is lived from a center point of inner integrity that reflects in my interactions with others and in my alone moments. No one has to tell me what integrity is because it is inherent within me. It speaks through my conscience and innate wisdom, keeping me attuned to the universal laws governing the universe.

Respect is at the heart of my motivations—respect for myself, for those in my family, my workplace, my spiritual community, my neighborhood, and my world. It is easy for me to extend this respect even to individuals whom I do not know but who are spiritually connected to me in the web of existence. This respect causes me to pour out a blessing on all life, to offer a prayer for the well-being of all.

The law of my life is generosity. I hold back nothing from life this day and attune myself to the inner guidance of the Spirit where I am to give of my time, energies, gifts, talents, and skills. I remain alert and am receptive to the people, places, and ways I am to share and circulate my resources.

Creativity is the order of my day. I set creative energy in motion from the moment I wake up, beginning with the way I prepare my consciousness, my mind, and my body to meet all that comes to me throughout this day. Where others see problems, I see creative solutions. Where there appears to be a lack of love, I am a delivery agent of love. In situations of miscommunication I bring the light of clarity. Creativeness is my nature, and it is my calling card.

Throughout this day I remember my spiritual manners and apply them liberally, with joy and enthusiasm.

## Notes

1. Pier M. Forni, *Choosing Civility: The Twenty-five Rules of Considerate Conduct* (New York: St. Martin's Press, Griffin, 2005).
2. Luke 6:31.

# 16
# Conscious Creativity:
## Heaven's Kiss of Inspiration

*Command my hands, what must they do*
*Command my life, it's here for you*
*God is the love that heals all creation*
*God is creator, makes all things new*
*and God needs us to shine its light*
*as me, as you*

Fires blazed before her altar. Magical potions were concocted to invoke her influence, bribes proffered for her favors. Courted more ardently than a courtesan, form and personality were given to her spirit in the mythologies of ancient cultures. Yet only those who enter the mystical inner realm unveil her mystique and stand in the presence of the celestial muse who stokes creativity: *Inspiration.*

Inspiration is the ingredient that distinguishes one creative effort from another. In the movie *Amadeus*, the life story of Mozart, the composer Antonio Salieri went mad from his jealous efforts to possess and destroy Mozart's creative spirit. But that which has received heaven's kiss of inspiration is infused with its immortal breath and therefore never dies. Mere human cleverness eludes the anointing touch of inspiration. What is birthed from the surface mind becomes a passing trend and lasts only until fickle humanity discards it as passé. Today, who thinks about the pet rock, the lava lamp, or the Macarena?

## INSPIRATION IS ATTUNEMENT WITH THE COSMIC CREATIVE PRINCIPLE

The cosmic ingredient that infused the creative genius of Walter Russell, George Washington Carver, Hildegard of Bingen, Rumi, Mirabai, Kabir, Walt Whitman, Kahlil Gibran, Beethoven, and countless others who so profoundly stir the human spirit is the inspiration that flowed into their awareness through their attunement with the Cosmic Creative Principle.

The key that unlocks the storehouse of conscious creativity is already within you. You turn the key with purifying practices such as meditation and interior prayer—techniques that cause a deep inner relaxation, a silencing of the ego, that place you in a state of openness and receptivity. As William Blake realized, when the "doors of perception are cleansed" we become sensitized to inspiration's knock at the door of our intuitive awareness. "Behold, I stand at the door and knock. If anyone hears My voice and opens the door, I will come in to him and dine with him, and he with Me."[1] These words of Jesus the Christ describe the state of union of the individual self with what some call God, Brahman, or the Universal One.

When we spiritually discern that the macrocosm—of which we are the microcosm—is the Source of our own creative process, we begin to participate in conscious co-creativity. This is our initiation into the spiritual understanding that we are on the planet to discover, cultivate, and deliver our gifts, talents, and skills.

## THE DIMENSIONS OF CREATIVE CONSCIOUSNESS

As a young spiritual seeker, I used to have a recurring dream about Johann Sebastian Bach. Now I wasn't exactly a Bach groupie, so I wondered why Johann was hanging out in my dream state instead of Jimi Hendrix. But there I was, dialoging with Mr. Bach about how to cultivate my creative potential for writing sacred music that would inspire and release the inner splendor of its listeners. Eventually the dreams stopped, but their memory lingered.

Some years later, I began my musical collaboration with Rickie Byars—now Rickie Byars Beckwith, my wife. Rickie and I conduct experiments in the laboratory of consciousness through meditation and prayer. When we are receptive to the muse of inspiration, it is as though all boundaries dissolve and we merge with the music, become the music itself. What Rickie and I have learned through this is that when you enter a genuine state of inspiration, you are literally breathed through by the very Spirit of Life.

Sometimes, in a lucid dream state, a direct contact with inspiration informs Rickie's music. In fact, not too long ago I myself dreamt about my spiritual brother, Carl Anderson, who passed away a few years ago. In my dream he was singing a song that, to the best of my ability, I then sang to Rickie. The minute I finished, she went downstairs to the piano and captured the melody as best she could. As I pen this chapter, we are devoting time to flesh out the gift that Carl gave us. Given that Carl was a consummate artist and very committed to the Agape spiritual community, we welcomed his input.

Insight sometimes occurs on the installment plan, so I was not surprised when reading *Talks with Great Composers* by Arthur M. Abell that I discovered the deeper significance of my nocturnal dialogues with Bach. (Through candid and lengthy personal interviews conducted, Abell captured the intimate, mystical details of how various composers dipped their consciousness into the living waters of inspiration.) "Where there is devotional music," Bach confided to Abell, "God is always at hand with His gracious presence." The great Johannes Brahms put it this way: "I will tell you about my method of communicating with the Infinite, for all truly inspired ideas come from God. I begin by appealing directly to my Maker, and straightaway the ideas flow in upon me, directly from God . . . You see, the powers from which all truly great composers drew their inspiration is the same power that enabled Jesus to work his miracles."[2]

## LIVING IN THE ZONE OF INSPIRATION

The mystics' raptures of divine love and the genius's works of art, music, poetry, literature, dance, and drama enthrall the human spirit with their excellence. Watching a basketball player make a seemingly miraculous jump shot, we may not at first attribute it to a mystically inspired state, thinking instead that the shot is the result of disciplined practice, superior physical abilities, or a special gift. However, during interviews, extraordinary athletes have talked about how they entered "the zone," an altered state wherein they experienced what resembles states of transcendence, as described by the mystics, which bestow a prowess beyond what is considered humanly possible. An inspired person can go beyond their ordinary state of consciousness, beyond mere intellect, technique, and willpower.

## RELEASE FALSE INHIBITIONS, PROHIBITIONS, AND EXHORTATIONS

Listening to a human voice reach a sublime note, reading poetry that breaks open the heart, witnessing a life selflessly dedicated to serving humanity, we are transported to a realm of awe. A surge of life energy rushes through us and we are inspired to tap into our own creativity. This sense of aliveness awakens within us an impulsion to cast off the ego's false inhibitions, prohibitions, and exhortations which sabotage the inner urge to self-express. Self-expression is so vital to our self-actualization that it caused psychologist and humanistic philosopher Erich Fromm to say, "I feel that the only thing that will save civilization ... is a renaissance of the spirit—a rebirth of the belief in man himself, in his essential creativeness."[3]

Failure to grasp the true nature of our life's purpose creates a spiritual identity crisis. Fortunately, in the reflecting pool of challenging experiences we begin to develop self-awareness. However, as Dr. Ernest Holmes, the founder of Religious Science, astutely observed, "Self-awareness without self-expression can almost as readily produce emotional disturbances as can the lack of self-awareness."[4] Pain pushes us until a higher vision for our life pulls us into creative self-expression. Each one of us is a co-creative agent with Spirit. Acceptance of our creative nature is the key to the inner vault of riches beyond our wildest imaginings! But to simply look at, hold, or place the key in the lock is not enough. We have to turn the key in order to enter the treasure house.

## WITH THREE TURNS OF THE KEY

### The first turn of the key occurs when you ask the perennial question, "Who am I?"

You cannot be your Authentic Self without becoming intimate with your true nature, without going beyond personality, cherished beliefs, likes, and dislikes. To discover your core Self, you must be willing to break the agreements you have made with mediocrity. The moment you stop running the racket of staying small to please society, family, friends, or bosses, your original face will start to come into focus and you will know who and what you really are as an emanation of the Universal One. As you come into an understanding of your true essence, you automatically want to know how you are to express it on the planet.

**The second turn of the key occurs when you ask yourself, "Why am I here?"**

There is an innate impulsion to know your purpose for being on the planet and to live it. We are not simply talking about your profession here but about your overarching purpose for having a human incarnation.

Following a recent speaking engagement, my wife and I were trying to catch an international flight that appeared to be logistically impossible to arrive for on time. After picking up our bags from the plane we just disembarked, we quickly headed to the next flight's check-in counter, discouraged by the long line we saw. Out of seemingly nowhere a sky cap attendant smilingly walked toward us. Imagine my surprise as the nearer he got I heard him quoting my words from the DVD *The Secret*, "You can start with nothing, and out of nothing and out of no way, a way will be made," followed by, "How can I serve you, Dr. Beckwith?" When I explained that we had to quickly navigate our check-in, he cheerfully said, "Don't worry about a thing."

He took our bags and our tickets. As we watched him walk towards the counter, he stopped to speak with a woman whose daughter was in a wheelchair. He asked the mother for permission to pray for her daughter, to which she agreed. He not only prayed for the daughter, he checked our bags and delivered our boarding passes, all with the utmost grace and ease. Obviously, he was a living demonstration of the words he quoted, because out of no way he became the way for us to make our flight. I knew that we were in the presence of an individual who knew that his real purpose on the planet was to be an angel of service, praying and serving as he fulfilled the responsibilities of his profession as a sky cap attendant.

With utmost sincerity ask within, "What is the Spirit's highest vision for my life?" When you ask such a question, you touch the heart of the Infinite, and when your intuition is attuned, you will receive a response. That response will have to do with generosity of spirit; it will have to do with the fact that your profession is only one of the vehicles through which you express your purpose and deliver your unique qualities of heart and spirit on the planet as only you can.

**The third turn of the key is your willingness to engage in a spiritual discipline, such as meditation.**

Meditation sensitizes your consciousness to receive divine guidance as it is whispered into your inner ear of intuition. The result is a conscious activation of your unique pattern of evolutionary unfoldment, which includes attunement with the creative muse of inspiration.

### EVERY ACT IS CREATIVE

The canvas of your life is very large and spacious. Your life circumstances are painted on this canvas in colors you have chosen through your conscious or unconscious use of the creative process. It is possible to turn what appear to be mundane activities—sweeping the street, cooking, washing dishes, changing diapers, mowing the lawn—into art forms. It was St. Augustine who said that you can identify a saintly being by the way they pick up an ordinary object, such as a pen. Spiritual attunement causes us to touch everything with ultimate respect, as an act of divine love and gratitude. Each of us is a candidate for living in such a precious way, for living such an elevated life.

These illuminating words of one of the world's most creative spirits, Albert Einstein, underscore the value of your contribution to the world: "It can easily be seen that all the valuable achievements, material and spiritual, which we receive from society have been brought about in the course of countless generations by creative individuals. Without creative personalities able to think and judge independently, the upward development is as unthinkable as the development of the individual personality without the nourishing soil of the community."[5]

In the consciousness of the Absolute there is no thought or act that is not creative. Indigenous cultures have always understood this. To this day, through prayer and ritual, they broadcast their call to the Spirit of Creativity present in all things. The Buddhist teaching of mindfulness powerfully illustrates how creativity courses through even the most normal, everyday activities. For example, the practice of mindful walking makes each step a creative act. As Ari Bloomekatz noted in the *L.A. Times* article, "The Seven Miracles of Mindfulness" on September 30th, 2007, the revered Zen master Thich Nhat Hanh teaches, "If we take steps without anxiety, in peace and joy, then we will cause a flower to bloom on the Earth with every step."

Western-oriented books on time management, so popular in our high-tech low-touch society, would no doubt find the practice of Buddhist mindfulness impractical. Materialistic thinking urges us to use downtime as an opportunity to create more to-do lists, update our site on YouTube, call our stockbroker from our cell phone, contact clients—anything to maximize each moment to make yet another dollar. After all, we've been raised on the maxim that "time is money." Our bodies are mindlessly put through the paces while our spirits are absent from mindful walking, cooking, eating, driving, or simply sitting. We are indoctrinated to perfect the art of one-upmanship for use on imaginary competitors. However, we are not here to live in an inner atmosphere of materialism and competition. We are here it live in a state of conscious creativity.

Entering a state of meditative awareness is a thoroughly creative act, for it is in a state of inner listening that we intuit the still, small voice announcing, revealing the creative presence within us. In an instant, in the gap between thoughts, a breakthrough may occur! The primordial sound of creation's cosmic song—the *Aum* of the Vedas, *Hum* of the Tibetans, *Amen* of the Judeo-Christians, and *Amin* of the Moslems—may rush our being with a surge of divine inspiration.

The Spirit of the living God is knocking at the door of your heart, reminding you that you are an exquisite, precious, and powerful being. Shine! Sing! Be bold enough to articulate what you are sensing, feeling, and knowing. Now is the time for you to partner with that immense power. Allow the tidal wave of the divine inspiration to wash over you and express in, through, and as you. Consciously and confidently enter the sacred process of co-creation, because That which expresses as you does not happen through anyone else in quite the same way. Become a master of your own divine, radiant creative expression.

### Affirmation

*I attune myself to the creative impulse that indwells me and seeks expression through me. I live to express my essential creativeness by performing every act mindfully, with the attentiveness of the artist that I am. My life is my canvas, and I cover it in acts of beauty, kindness, generosity, and authentic self-expression.*

### Embodiment

Creativity works through me in elegant ways, causing me to fully express in all of my outward and inward acts. The Spirit within me knows no limits to my creative expression and directs me in all my ways, in every aspect of my life.

I activate creativity in this word I speak on my own behalf, knowing that it pours through me as the limitless inspiration of my mind, the generosity of my heart, the appreciation I feel for the beauty that indwells and surrounds me.

Today, I consciously turn the key to the treasure house of my inner being. Through meditation and affirmative prayer I attune myself to my true nature. Any agreements that I have made in the past with mediocrity, any excuses I have used to postpone fully expressing my essential self are now broken, dissolved, and return to the nothingness from which they came. I confidently step into a larger dimension of myself, into the co-creative genius that I now know myself to be.

When I ask the Spirit within, "What is my highest purpose?" I hear its answer in language my heart can understand and respond to. I take action on the intuitive guidance I receive and am faithful to it.

I declare my willingness, my receptivity, and my enthusiasm to enter a conscious, co-creative relationship with the Spirit. This statement of truth breaks through any seeming obstruction, every stubborn attempt to cover my creativity by remaining small. Clarity, confidence, and commitment go before me.

My universe is alive with creativity in the smallest and the grandest actions I perform. I am upheld, maintained, guided, and inspired by the very Source of creativity itself. What a sweet relationship it is! I have complete trust in this indwelling power and give thanks for it. In all situations I behold the power of the Spirit unfolding and expressing in, as, and through me. Its love and goodness fill my inner and outer environment. I do not seek these qualities because I know they are already mine. I simply give thanks for them and let it be.

## Notes

1. Revelation 3:20.
2. Arthur M. Abell, *Talks with Great Composers: Candid Conversations with Brahms, Puccini, Strauss, and Others* (New York: Philosophical Library, 1955).
3. Eric Fromm, *The Art of Being* (London: Continuum International Publishing Group, 1994).
4. Ernest Holmes, *Words That Heal Today: A Science of Mind Book* (New York: Dodd Mead, 1988).
5. Albert Einstein, *The World as I See It* (Secaucus, N.J.: Citadel Press, 1993).

# 17
# Soulware for Authentic Happiness

*My prayer today is for the courage to be*
*What the Holy Spirit intends for me*
*I want to be better an opening for God to*
*Make me stronger*

As human beings, we have a sense of entitlement where happiness is concerned and with good reason: happiness is our true nature. The meaning of happiness and how to experience it has been explored by the world's spiritual traditions, philosophy, psychology, and even science. Yet few are those who realize that the soulware for happiness was installed within us the moment we came into existence.

Most individuals do not penetrate deeply enough into their core essence to touch their true nature of happiness. Instead, they are content to remain on the surface, looking everywhere outside of themselves to "find" what has never been lost. They let the dictates of society, religion, celebrities, media, advertising, and television do the work of defining happiness and how it may be experienced. As long as this is the depth of an individual's seeking, only disappointment can result. We realize happiness at the level of our understanding of happiness.

In your search for happiness, it is helpful to become clear about whether or not you are pursuing authentic happiness or its shadow: pseudo pleasure. Happiness vendors should be carefully assessed to determine whether or not their product—be it a spiritual teacher or organization, book, workshop, or healing modality—contains the ingredients that provide more than superficial, temporary results.

When beginning a spiritual path, it is common to realize, perhaps for the first time, that the sources of happiness we have been taught to believe in and encouraged to pursue lack deep roots. The benefit of such an insight is that we become more compassionate about the growing pains we encounter as we evolve into a more spiritually mature understanding of happiness. We also catch how our culture is happiness-addicted in that the slightest amount of disappointment or sadness is diagnosed as depression, and prescription drugs are the solution. In truth, a temporary state of unhappiness may be feedback from the Universe that it's time to introspect and see how our life-choices are causing or preventing us from manifesting our natural state of joy.

### HAPPINESS IS A CHOICE

Happiness cannot be forced upon us nor can we force it upon others. Each individual must give his or her consent to being happy. Any day of the week, we can learn about people who maintain their zest for life amidst circumstances that are anything but happy. "How did she do that?" we ask, simultaneously sizing up ourselves about how we would respond in such a situation. When we download our happiness soulware, we activate the deep roots of joy within the human spirit that transcend external conditions.

Choosing happiness as a way of life ultimately leads to the understanding that joy is our natural state of being. Happiness is not simply when plans going according to our ego's desires, such as getting a bonus at work, a new credential after our name, fame or fortune. As wonderful as these experiences are, they provide only temporary satisfaction. A good example is when we buy a new car. For weeks after we drive our prized possession off the lot, we enjoy that pleasurable aroma of "newness" that hits the olfactory nerves each time we enter our vehicle. Soon enough, however, that pleasant fragrance turns into the smell of stale mocha latte, and we are back to looking for a fresh replacement that we think will once again make us happy.

Considering all the challenges we currently face in our world, happiness may seem a frivolous and even selfish endeavor. We cannot deny global tragedies—any meaningful discussion about happiness cannot ignore the pains of war, genocide, oppression, AIDS, poverty, and starvation. It can be confounding when we examine the lives of individuals who have made and continue to make a tremendous impact in forwarding the causes of justice and peace on the planet and find that their circumstances in life may be far from the common concept of happiness. Paradoxical as it may seem, inner joy can be experienced in the midst of extraordinary challenges. To accept and work with this paradox is a practice of the spiritually and psychologically mature.

## HAPPINESS: ITS CAUSES AND EFFECTS

Genuine happiness begins when we become conscious that we are co-creators of our destiny with life's source, whether we call it God, the Universal One, or no name at all. Authentic happiness does not come from outer sources; it comes from an inner realization of the Self.

Our soulware for happiness is downloaded through meditation, affirmative prayer, spiritual study, visioning, contemplation, and sacred service. These practices re-groove our habitual thought patterns and enable us to make wisdom-guided, happiness-producing choices. We continue to enjoy the outer pleasures of human existence, and also seek the unconditional happiness that comes from going homeward within to our soul-source.

When we demand that the law of attraction fulfill the desires of our entitled ego, it doesn't take long to realize that authentic happiness refuses to bow to our spiritual materialism. The saying "Be careful what you pray for because you just might get it" is another way of encouraging us to be discerning about that for which we pray, because when it manifests, we may have to pray again to have it removed from our life. The imaginary halo of happiness we place around those material things that we are convinced will bring us joy becomes tarnished by the reality of their powerlessness to fulfill us. For example, if your concept of happiness is owning a TV screen that is bigger than your vision for your life, what will happen if the TV breaks down and you have lost the source of your happiness?

## THE FOUR "Cs" OF HAPPINESS

There are areas of life in which we participate that utilize our happiness soulware. I call them the four Cs of happiness: conversation, company, challenges, and commitment, which change the contents of our consciousness. For simplicity's sake, we can call the four Cs "causes," and the way in which they change the contents of our consciousness "effects."

### Conversation: vibrational heaven or hell?

Developing an awareness of the power of words and their energetic effect is a spiritual practice that is not necessarily easy. In social and personal situations, we so often find ourselves swept into the lowest common denominator of conversation so that we can fit in or not take a stand against the prevailing popular opinion.

If you are prone to gossiping and complaining, you will see the world according to the contents of that level of conversation and impair the soulware of happiness from flowing through you. In contrast, if the energy-content of your conversations consists of encouragement, compassion, constructive advice when sought, you will be a vehicle of wise insight and awareness while simultaneously activating your happiness soulware.

To illustrate the vibrational power of language, consider two little words that we use countless times throughout the day: "yes" and "no." Since early childhood these words have been part of our lexicon and inform the parenting of our own children.

When "yes" or "no" are directed *at* us, seldom are we neutral. We rejoice or recoil, enter a mental heaven or hell depending upon our expectations, projections, and interpretations. When these words rise up in our throat, aim, and hit their target, we have emotional backup in defense of their appropriateness. The vibration of these two words as energies of acceptance, rejection, or release exercises a potent influence upon us. What if I were to tell you that "yes" and "no" are equals on the playing ground of their synonym, "affirm"? Language can be paradoxical, so there are times when "yes" actually means "no" and when "no" means "yes." And sometimes when we say "no" in response to a request, we may be casting a vote of "yes" on behalf of our own well-being.

Personality manipulation techniques made popular in "how-to" books instruct us how to get what we want from others while we seemingly remain politically, socially, professionally, romantically, or spiritually correct. These practices come at a high cost, because no technique can manipulate the true power of happiness. Often we are taught to cloak our meaning in "nice" words instead of being authentic. The effect? We become divided against ourselves. Our motivations and intentions determine the integrity of our speech. Our speech, in turn, determines our inner state of happiness.

How are we to develop a relationship of congruency in our inner and outer conversations? How does one practice the spiritual principle of right speech and its complement, listening? We start by examining the quality of our conversations within our own minds.

What is the quality of your self-conversations? What comes out of your mouth when you talk to people who are your intimates, your colleagues, your children, your family, your friends, and those you may consider rivals or competitors? What is the quality of your nonverbal speech—the vibration you emit through your thoughts? We may benefit from the words of the Psalmist to "Set a guard over my mouth O Lord; keep watch over the door of my lips" and take it a bit further by understanding that even our nonverbal conversation impacts our state of consciousness and therefore all those around us.[1]

In my own introspection, I have found that by setting the intention to speak and listen with awareness I become attuned to intuitive guidance from within. Renunciation of an attachment to speaking and listening creates a vibration in consciousness that guides me to know the appropriateness of what to say to whom, why, when, and where. Perfect conversation is not the goal—awareness is. The more awareness we bring to our intention to consciously converse and listen, the more sensitivity we have about how the vibration of our words affects us and others. Our conversations then take on the graciousness born of an inner life lived in communion with the still, small voice that ever whispers within, activating our soulware for happiness.

### Company: keeping it holy

The second "C" at the root of our happiness is the company we keep. When you choose a friend, you are biting off a chunk of your own destiny. When friends come together and through their individualized states of consciousness impact one another, they have the power to alter the course of their destinies through their energetic exchanges.

Who are you running with? Who are your homies? Do you bring out the best in one another? As parents, we are watchful of the company our children keep, but are we equally vigilant about our own? As adults, we sometimes think that we're beyond being influenced by our company. With all due respect for the beauty of each person's individuality, what quality of consciousness predominates in your network of friends? What shared values, goals, and activities form your bonds? Do you inspire and uplift one another? Do you create a climate of joy when you are together? Is honesty and open communication encouraged? Until you have become grounded in your growth and development practices, it is good to be aware of what arises in your mind, heart, and actions in the company you keep.

The benefits of interacting with individuals within a spiritual community are many. Spiritual community, or *sangha* as it is known in Sanskrit, is one of the Buddha's three jewels of existence. We can look into the mirror of our community and learn many things about ourselves from what is reflected back to us. When we go through a period of discouragement, our community of spiritual practitioners inspires and reminds us of our spiritual intention to wake up. Our clarity and confidence are recharged and we re-attune to our happiness soulware. When a community gathers together to meditate, pray, study, and serve, an alchemical process occurs that accelerates the evolutionary process of all who are present.

### Challenges: maps to your inner growth

Sometimes we believe that we want to live a challenge-free life, and yet something within us knows that in spite of their annoyance factor, challenges are great awakeners. Challenges disrupt our cherished paradigms and opinions, causing us to open our consciousness and let in new thoughts, ideas, perceptions, and points of view. Sometimes, the bigger the challenge the bigger the insight and resulting happiness. The truth is that there is no escape from challenges. We can perhaps postpone or resist a particular challenge for a while, but eventually it will become impossible for us to not look it in the face and grow through it.

Welcome challenges. Let them interrupt your familiar mindscape. Don't waste your time praying away challenges because that isn't a constructive approach. Welcome them, make friends with them. Use affirmative prayer to declare that your inner treasure house is equipped with all that you need to meet your current challenge. In this way, you will grow into the realization that challenges help you to unleash your highest potential. If you read the biographies or autobiographies of individuals who have made a significant contribution to the planet, you will realize that their lives were anything but challenge-free. Their challenges provided the context for the discovery and expression of their profoundest gifts.

In Lewis Carroll's *Alice in Wonderland*, the queen advises us to believe at least six impossible things before breakfast. This is wisdom, because the courage to challenge ourselves is what brings about a paradigm shift that increases our happiness quotient. Most people are unconsciously attached to remaining in the tight cocoon of security they have woven, imagining that it keeps them safe from life's challenges. However, when we courageously welcome challenges, we are ushered into deeper realizations, awakenings, and thereby into authentic happiness.

Courage comes from the Old French *corage*, which means "heart" and "spirit." It is the mark of the spiritual warrior who, in spite of the unknown that lies ahead, continues to take the risk of moving forward. In everyday life, courage is turning off the television and iPod, shutting down the laptop and other entertainment in order to sit in your own company long enough to become self-acquainted with who and what you are. It is being with yourself long enough to make friends with all that you see about yourself. And I do mean *all.* Courage is to risk being authentic.

Courageous individuals do not moralistically compartmentalize life into that which is acceptable and that which is unacceptable. A spiritually mature individual is discerning yet nonjudgmental. In Thea Alexander's novel *2150 A.D.*, one of her protagonists astutely shares that "the measure of a mind's evolution is its acceptance of the unacceptable. What may be unacceptable at the micro level is always acceptable at the Macro level. Remember that everything is perfect from a Macro view, remember that nothing is terrible from a Macro view. Things can only be terrible from the micro perspective, which is too limited to see that we live in a perfectly just and balanced macrocosm in which we experience only what we have chosen."[2] In the macrocosm, there is only order; only in the microcosm do we see chaos due to faulty vision. If we could step back far enough we would see an underlying order. In other words, beneath every human aberration there is a spiritual aspiration.

Courage is not the absence of fear. Courage acknowledges fear and is fearless about it. When we are courageous, we are open, vulnerable to the *new* being interwoven into the fabric of our being. When we embrace the new, we create an opening for grace to make its home in us. Courage accelerates our transformation and expands our happiness quotient.

**Commitment: the hallmark of freedom**

Be honest. Fess up. The ego in each of us tries to convince us that we are more spiritually awake than we actually are. Spiritual arrogance is insidiously deceptive. It comes about, in part, by the seduction of spiritual paths that have guaranteed us "instant enlightenment" or techniques that enable us to "meditate like a Buddhist monk in just twenty minutes!"

The ego loves hearing that the path of transformation doesn't have to be challenging. Who doesn't like hearing that we need only believe—not *do* any inner work—to become spiritually awake? The inspiration of words is easier to accommodate than the perspiration of practice. After all, affirming that you are part and parcel of God does not require the same discipline as what it takes to *realize* your God Consciousness. And if reincarnation is part of your belief system, you may think, "What's the rush when I have as many lives as it takes to become enlightened?"

We don't want to become spiritual junkies running from seminar to seminar quoting their teachers but practicing nothing. Going on pilgrimages to exotic "power spots" can inspire us but cannot take the place of the simple commitment to take a seat under the bodhi tree of our own consciousness and face the sometimes-boredom and sometimes-bliss of meditation practice. Plenteous are the excuses we make for not committing to do what it takes to awaken to our inherently enlightened state of being.

Wise commitments do not bind us, they free us. To the spiritually immature, *commitment* is a very scary word because it is internalized as bondage. But to the spiritually mature, commitment is the equivalent of freedom because it bestows authentic happiness that cannot be taken away. When you make an unconditional commitment to your spiritual practice, the energy response from the universe matches you at the point of your commitment. And grace is always in service to the sincerely committed practitioner.

**Consciousness: the ability to be aware that you are aware**

The word *consciousness* is thrown about so casually that it's easy to lose sight of what it means, even more so when it is defined as being "awakened." Awakened consciousness is a state of being aware that you are aware. It is a realization that you are the watcher, the witness within you—not the analyzer, not the thinker, not even the meditator, but that which is the impartial witness of every aspect of your being and doing.

When you consciously realize that you are the watcher, you are freed from the narrow confines of outer labels: male, female, Asian, Caucasian, Black, gay, straight, vegetarian, carnivore, Republican, Democrat, Christian, Hindu, Taoist, and so on. These must crumble in order for your true identity as pure consciousness to emerge. Beliefs, concepts, and perceptions are the *contents* of consciousness, but they are not consciousness itself. We know they are not consciousness because they can be changed, shifted, transformed. Consciousness itself is an "isness" that is the changeless, formless, ever-existing aspect of your being that is not influenced by anything external. *What is vital to your spiritual understanding is that you are empowered to evolve the contents of your consciousness into alignment with consciousness itself.* As you do so, the contents of your consciousness change their vibratory frequency, causing a resultant shift in the outer circumstances of your life.

You want to keep the contents of your consciousness attuned to the harmonious flow of life, to the laws governing the universe. As you catch the realization that your consciousness is limitless, you will realize that "I am here to live beyond self-imposed boundaries, to break through the flimsily constructed ceilings on my experience of life." You will then participate in the co-creative dance of life, not as a successful problem-solver but as an individual who is taking full possession of your spiritual inheritance of joy, love, harmony, and creativity. You are not here to merely survive but to soar, to express and release the dynamic power of consciousness residing at the deepest center of your being.

Each of us stands on the platform of our own unique evolutionary pattern of unfoldment, fully empowered to wake up. Let us all become lionhearted spiritual warriors knowing that right on the ground where we now stand we may apply our soulware of happiness and uplift ourselves and all beings.

### Affirmation

*The cosmic laughter of Spirit bathes my soul in joy. I see with clear seeing, and all that I do is from the pure joy of being. I love life and I love living. I love being me as I am me.*

### Embodiment

I consciously choose happiness as a way of life. I saturate my mind with joy, the joy that comes from within. I am now one with this joy. It informs my thoughts and emotions and acts through me. Joy upholds me, blesses me, inspires me. I am intoxicated with the joy of pure being.

My trust in my co-creative relationship with the Spirit guides my every thought and action. My conversations are honest, affirmative, uplifting, and loving. I use my words wisely, knowing that the vibration they carry impacts my consciousness and those with whom I speak.

The company I keep enhances my life. We are a mutual source of encouragement, support, and nurturance to one another. In the heart of my friends I see a reflection of myself, the ways in which I have grown and have yet to grow. The strength of support that I give and receive enables me to share and serve where the Spirit leads me.

As a spiritual warrior, courage lights my path with the ability to walk into the unknown with confidence, with trust in the fundamental goodness of the universe. I am fearless about my fear. I embrace courage and transform fear into my friend. I willingly take risks by opening myself to being vulnerable to change, by getting to know myself through and through without judgment or egoic pride in my accomplishments.

Challenges reveal the inner work I am to do, and I welcome them. My greatest desire is to awaken the watcher within me that knows and knows that it knows, that has known since the beginning of time that I am a limitless, eternal being. Challenges are the calling card of transformation, and I courageously enter them knowing that they are the rich material for my awakening.

The Universal One has given fully of itself to me. My trust in it forms the deep roots of my courage that transmutes doubt, worry, and fear into peace and joy. This is my commitment to myself, my contract with my inner spirit, my spiritual practices, my teachers, and my spiritual community. I honor my commitment as an act of self-responsibility. Today is brightened with the light of my spiritual agreement with my Oversoul. I am awake and aware of all that I am committed to and act accordingly. The very power of this word transforms the contents of my consciousness, and I give thanks for it.

## Notes

1. Psalm 141:3.
2. Thea Alexander, *2150 A.D.* (New York: Warner Books, Inc., 1976).

# 18
# How to Make It through the Night:
## A Luminous View of the Dark Night of the Soul

*You have got to stand*
*When you're feeling hopeless*
*and vision has been tossed upon*
*a stormy sea*
*Joy is there in your soul*
*Get on up and stand and say*
*God is enough for me*

The fine print of spiritual awakening cannot ignore those times known as the dark night of the soul. This concluding chapter will clarify how spiritually beneficial the dark night is to those who are deeply committed to their self-realization.

This night is like no other. It is inescapable, even desirable, for those who sincerely desire the transforming touch of the Spirit. This night—which can last moments, days, weeks, even years—feels like the bottom has fallen out of our lives. Our friends and family don't understand what we are going through, and whatever compassion they offer can't reach the depth of our despair. The spiritual path we're following has become as dry as dust and clearly isn't working.

To an individual accustomed to living in conscious communion with the Ineffable, this dark night is an excruciating dry spell without a trace of divine succor. The density of the external world presses itself against your soul, weighing heavily upon your heart. Maybe God isn't real after all and enlightenment is just fiction. There's no inner direction in sight and you feel completely alone. Agonizing emotions of the egoic structure convince you that you are not going to survive this hopeless state of being, that you are going to die, and that if you did, it would be okay.

### YOU'RE IN GOOD COMPANY

The dark night experience is far different from ordinary sadness, depression, or anxiety. It is the profound experience referred to in the mystical traditions as the dark night of the soul, the great spiritual catalyst that threatens to shatter the ego and a sense of a self separate from the Whole. In such circumstances, all we want to know is, how do I make it through the night?

Every mystic, sage, or awakened master whose autobiography or biography I have read has experienced the dark night of the soul. In fact, once having experienced the gifts of the dark night, they actually prayed for it! St. John of the Cross, a Carmelite monk from the sixteenth-century, is perhaps the most sublime of all Spanish mystics. His book, *Dark Night of the Soul*, is a valuable guide for navigating the dark night, a classic in mystical literature. In one stanza he writes, "O dark night, kindled in love with yearnings—oh happy chance!" Again he writes, "The endurance of darkness is preparation for great light."[1] His words reveal the seeming polarity of the dark and light sides of incubating in the emptiness-fullness of it all—empty of all that we desire and full of that which we find repugnant. When you're experiencing a dark night, read about the life of an illumined being and you will realize that you are in good company.

### SOUL-ACTIVITY OF THE DARK NIGHT

While it seems more natural than unnatural to reject the dark night experience, one does so at the expense of a profound purification in consciousness. Being caught between two worlds—one's current way of being and birthing the next level of awareness—we wonder if the spiritual benefits will even come close to outweighing the grueling pain of sticking it out. When we deeply surrender to the spiritual life, we come face-to-face with the discovery that no matter how much we think we know, we actually know very little. We went to bed thinking we knew something and woke up saying, "I . . . I . . . I don't know anything." A gauntlet is thrown down in the face of ego. Remember, a bad day for the ego is a good day for the soul!

We may have read countless spiritual books, sat at the feet of many spiritual masters, gone on pilgrimages to all the spiritual hot spots, and still have inwardly realized very little. Maybe we've been hanging out in high intellectualism and metaphysical conversations thinking we're paragons of spiritual knowledge. Hopefully we've reached the point of wisdom where we are humble enough to admit we still know very little. This is called "positive ignorance," because it demonstrates an open and teachable inner attitude which humbly acknowledges that there remains a distance to go in arriving at self-realization, along with the understanding that our journey of becoming is limitless, unending.

It's important to understand that the dark night is not a matter of outer desires in life that aren't going our way. It is not unfed egoic satisfaction that the law of attraction is not working for us. It is not a temper tantrum with a spiritual label of "dark night." For example, we don't get the part we auditioned for and we're behind in the rent. Or a loan we were counting on didn't come through. The right relationship just isn't demonstrating for us. Those are not the "dark nights" I'm talking about. *Profound movements in consciousness that unravel the entanglements of ego, experiences that literally or metaphorically bring us to our knees and take us through a seeming disintegration so that we may experience reintegration at a higher level of consciousness—these are dark nights of the soul.*

The dark night reveals the subterranean soul-activity of which the external circumstance is just a symptom. It is a gift to the soul that provides the teaching which becomes the cosmic doorway through which we take a closer step to spiritual awakening. *Darkness and light are both part of our journey. Darkness is the depth of spiritual potential hidden in the void of infinite possibility. Light is the manifestation of that potential in the external dimension of time and space.*

## THE DARK NIGHT HAPPENS TO THOSE WHO QUALIFY FOR IT

The dark night of the soul occurs within individuals who mean business with their spiritual practice, individuals who have made a profound commitment to evolve and awaken. One must be spiritually qualified in consciousness for such a profound experience because it is not simply a "spiritually romantic" notion, a spiritual soap opera to write a libretto about. I speak from experience when I say that a dark night experience puts an end to your life as you know it, including those parts you would like to cling to and never have changed. But when you mean business with the Spirit, it means business with you, and a re-qualification of consciousness ensues.

It is impossible to manipulate our way out of the dark night, even though the ego seeks to do so in its attempt to maintain an appearance of control. There are no spiritual endorphins we may swallow that offer relief once we say "yes" and surrender to the mystical process taking place within us. But the ego doesn't give up without a fight.

One of the ego's mechanisms is to become involved in compulsive behaviors such as overdrinking, serial dating, drugs, or shopping. When you analyze it, you see you are trying to avoid yourself and relieve your present-moment experience of fear, loneliness, anxiety. Continuing in these escape mechanisms may lead to the development of an addictive behavior that provides a temporary high. However, we are not here to get high; we are here to become conscious and free.

Another of the ego's rackets is the wishful thinking syndrome: "I wish I were someone else," we lament, "somewhere else, experiencing something else—*anything but this!*" Such an attitude has no transformative value at all, nor does mentally or verbally screaming positive affirmations in order to bypass the darkness we are facing, to drown out the scary inner voice that says, "Pssst, hey, you're not okay!"

To the Spirit, light and dark are equal; there is no separation, no difference. Some of my favorite sources of encouragement during a dark night experience are these verses from the 139th Psalm: "If I ascend into heaven, You are there; If I make my bed in hell, behold, You are there. If I take wings of the morning, and dwell in the uttermost parts of the sea, even there Your hand shall lead me. And Your right hand shall hold me. If I say, 'Surely the darkness shall fall on me,' even the night shall be light about me. Indeed, the darkness shall not hide from You, but the night shines as the day; The darkness and the light are both alike to You. For you formed my inward parts: You covered me in my mother's womb. I will praise You, for I am wonderfully made."[2]

You will find it challenging to accept that a dark night of the soul has in fact been called forth from deep within you by the indwelling Knower. Trust that it recognizes exactly what is needed to command forth in you authentic empowerment, unconditional love, compassion, clarity, humility, and strength, to name just a few of the dark night's grace-filled blessings.

Resisting or trying to short-circuit this transformational process prevents us from reaping the fullness of its fruitage.

Opening ourselves to it, entering it fully and feeling all of its textures allows us to outwit the ego's illusory game and catch a deeper understanding of where it is lovingly and wisely leading us. As we willingly surrender ourselves to the evolutionary process of the dark night, placing no time demands upon it, we make ourselves available to profound transformation.

### PRACTICES FOR NAVIGATING THE DARK NIGHT

One way to handle the ego's illusory game is to begin your own inner dialogue of spiritual inquiry: "If this dark night never goes away, what quality would I have to cultivate to have peace of mind? What am I being guided to release from my habitual pattern of being—my surface personality—so that I may evolve to my next level of awareness?"

Perhaps the quality being called forth is love, forgiveness, compassion, unselfishness, patience, humility, nonattachment, trust, generosity of heart, perseverance, or lovingkindness for yourself. The moment you stop resisting the dark night, you create a condition for this quality to rise up from within you and take hold in your consciousness. Then your attention is diverted from getting rid of your discomfort and is redirected toward accelerating your transformation. Rather than seeking relief from what you are experiencing, place your attention on the quality that is trying to emerge in your awareness, even as you simultaneously embrace your discomfort, whether it's fear, doubt, anger—whatever it is. These emotions cannot consume you because they are not your true nature. Face them with soul-confidence and you will ultimately intuit the quality that you are being called to birth and express.

Meditation and prayer reverse the searchlight of awareness from our limited experience of ourselves to our unlimited Self.

Suddenly, what was so devastatingly painful becomes more acceptable. We begin to catch the beauty in our experience. Tangible evidence is given through our own unique romance with the Infinite that something valuable and profound is taking place. *What was perceived as a hole in our soul is understood to be a contribution that makes us whole*. We become motivated to reach down deep and become acquainted with a more profound aspect of who and what we are. A moment of total ego collapse reveals all the ways that we've been manipulating, controlling and coaxing circumstances to go our way. We understand that these rackets no longer serve us. How liberating to realize that no external circumstance can permanently cover the innate radiance of the soul! Nothing can permanently obliterate our true identity. No temporary experience can forever camouflage the beauty of our being.

Another valuable practice when dark night seems to embrace eternity is to ask yourself, "Where and how can I give of myself? *Where can I begin to express and radiate?*" Just scan your awareness and allow for guidance to present itself. Search within for a quality you may begin to pour forth upon others, one that causes a bigger opening in consciousness. Even if you receive no clear sense of direction, reach beyond your current inner experience and give of yourself. This causes a soul-expansion to occur so that where you were constricted you begin to expand, where you were withholding you now choose to give. This breaks the stronghold of the egoic mind's grip on our human frailties. Punitive thoughts like, "I've made a mistake and I'm now paying for it; this must be my karma; or who's to blame for this?" become neutralized. A new order of mental and emotional reaction to our experience of the dark night then begins to establish itself within our consciousness.

Letting go of the judging mind that labels our experience as one of lack, pain, limitation, frustration, failure, confusion, or aridity in our spiritual practices is accomplished through selfless service. When in the midst of what we are going through we ask, "*Where may I give of myself in service to others?*" we expand beyond the little egoic self and merge into the freedom that is found in the larger Self. In the movement of giving of ourselves somewhere—it doesn't matter where—that Great Something within us that remains untouched, unmoved by our experience begins to be activated. We then see ourselves from a more expansive and generous vantage point. We see qualities come forth from ourselves that express the true dignity and elegance of our character.

Expanding beyond the narrow confines of resistance to the dark night causes something within to break through the habitual mental pattern that's holding you hostage. A shift takes place. You will see yourself anew. You will begin to walk taller in the awareness that the morning always follows the night.

## REMEMBERING TO REMEMBER

I appreciate Dr. Howard Thurman's reminder that during a dark period we have the opportunity to learn how to walk in "remembered radiance." We all have moments when we have felt wholly connected to life. Those moments become eclipsed when we enter the dark night. But when we bring this remembered radiance into our awareness, we know that it has not permanently been lost. When we understand the play of light and dark in our life we know we are on a grand path of the heart. Our perception of ourselves changes, as it must when the activity of the Spirit flows through us.

As we give of ourselves we are literally forced into seeing the Good within us. This right seeing allows us to realize, honor, and appreciate our unique pattern of unfoldment. We cease comparing ourselves to others and leave behind any sense of inferiority or superiority. Our relationship with the Infinite becomes intimate and personal to us. We trust where the Spirit is leading us and bless the dark night of the soul for illuminating our path. This impress of the Self upon the self is what is called making it through the night. Walk into it with full confidence and trust.

### Affirmation

*I surrender to the alchemy of the dark night of the soul. I give my consent to its transforming touch and am patient in the midst of my discomfort. I am open, receptive, and resist not. Even now I sense the soul-activity taking place within me and am grateful for it.*

### Embodiment

No longer do I struggle against uncomfortable circumstances, feelings, and experiences in which I cannot see an immediate way out. I listen to their message and receive their gifts. When all seems dark, I know that I am in a development process that is guided and lighted by the Spirit within. I go forward in confidence and trust.

I respond to the inner call of my spirit to go deeper within, to allow its transforming touch to reveal my wholeness. Something new is being born within me, and I yield to it.

Meditation may be difficult and my prayers seem dry, and even this I surrender.

The Spirit within me knows what it is doing with my life. Darkness and light are the same—both give birth to my awakening. I am willing to become more myself through this process. My inner perception shifts, and I welcome this experience. I embrace it.

These words that I speak are my declaration of rebirth. It is active within me now and something magnificent is happening. Something rich is happening. With complete assurance, I know that the Spirit is for me and not against me, that Life is for me and not against me. I am a child of the universe, here to learn to walk in love of God amidst the crash of breaking worlds. I say, "This shall not move me," and it does not. I am divinely supported, and all things work together for my good.

**Notes**

1. St. John of the Cross, *Dark Night of the Soul* (Mineola, N.Y.: Dover Publications, 2003).
2. Psalm 139: 8–14.

# Afterword

Rarely do I read something and agree with every word! With this magnificent book by Michael Bernard Beckwith, that is truly the case. Not that I am not startled and surprised by some of his statements, moved and stirred by them. Not that some of them do not push me along beyond lesser habits of mind. Not that I do not sense that there is more to some of them than I can immediately comprehend. I read and, through his fresh perspective, I learn new things—and new ways of experiencing familiar things.

Take, for example, the way he brings non-duality and love together, as they should be—not merely as abstract concepts but as fundamental to an enlightened life.

What does he mean by "non-dual," one of my favorite words too, very essential in Indian spirituality, Hinduism as well as Buddhism? "Non-dual" means that God as Universal Love, Buddha as Universal Compassion, are here with us right now. Mega-Agape and Maha-Karuna are the reality here and now. Our habitually perceived world of unkindness, insufficiency, danger, and suffering is real to us, but fortunately not as real as God's love or Buddha's compassion. This really is fortunate, since it means that we are already "saved," "liberated" by a power greater than our own misperception.

Love in Buddha's Sanskrit means "will to the happiness of the beloved," and compassion means "will to end the suffering of the beloved"—two sides of the same coin. Therefore, this vision that Christ's and Buddha's love and compassion are the ground-level energy of the universe, this vision is a huge relief, however much of it we can glimpse, initially through reasonable belief and eventually through deep understanding.

Every word on every page of *Spiritual Liberation* exudes this deeper awareness of the loving energy of which our beings are intricately woven.

In the flow of that awareness, Michael reveals himself to set us an example. He holds nothing back, shares his trials and tribulations, his agonies and joys. His evident delight in living in a vibrant oneness in his own individual way overflows to lift us also up into our own particular embrace of oneness.

We first met at his Agape International Spiritual Center, one joyful Sunday. He spoke on the theme of "All Right Already." He soared over and through his community, who themselves were overwhelmingly sweet and affirming, and I was moved to tears. *A-gaa-pey* is Greek for "love," as the flowing happiness of communion in the abundance of liberating and sustaining energy that is the clear light freedom ground of every universe.

His theme was that we are all-right all-ready, not just rushing elsewhere to escape our suffering, presuming that freedom and well-being await us when we someday get there. No! The word is, Heaven is within us, we are not to live in fear and worry. He quoted Jesus' statement about how to deal with "trials and tribulations"—whatever happens, just "Be of good cheer!" Where do we find the good cheer even under duress? From within, from the heavenly resource of energy we are made of.

Shantideva, the great Indian Buddhist sage and saint, spoke in a similar way, to this effect: If you can do something about a bad situation, why be angry about it? Just do it! If you can't do anything about it, why hurt yourself more by getting angry about it? Frustration is the fuel of bitterness and anger. Remain cheerful and you stay free, no matter what happens, life or death.

In this amazing book, Michael also teaches us how to evolve in freedom toward our full potential.

A sentence of his particularly jumped out at me, when he is describing "transformation" as something beyond self-improvement or change. "Transformation occurs when identification with the egoic self is dropped through a conscious realization of the Authentic Self." This is totally in consonance with the Jewish, Christian, and Sufi mystics and is technically corroborated by Indic psychologies of Hinduism and Buddhism. What Michael calls "Authentic Self" is called "Supreme Self" by Hindus and "Selfless Self" by Buddhists, meaning precisely the authentic liberated self free of the egoic self.

Throughout this wonderful book, Michael's encouraging words open the door for us into the non-dual, evolutionary, fulfilled life. It is spiritual liberation for sure. And the more people who awaken to this abundance of being, the more kind they will be to each other (and to other beings, of course) and the more happy the world will be. It is an endless process perhaps, but it is all happening in the now, the infinite now, into which Michael leads us again and again, in chapter after chapter, affirmation after affirmation, embodiment after embodiment.

Finally, one passage touched me especially closely, as it concerned my friend and mentor His Holiness the Dalai Lama. I was impressed by the clarity of Michael's perception. "What I admired on that occasion was how the Dalai Lama openly expressed his feelings about the suffering of the Tibetan people, whom he profoundly loves, and how in the next instant a smile of transcendence would light up his face. Even as he spoke out against what is happening in his country, he was not entrapped by that experience. He did not freeze-frame the scene. In his wisdom he realized that life is fluid, that those who suffer today can be free tomorrow. He pierced the veil of appearances and saw Reality. I attribute this in great measure to his daily discipline of meditation, which gives him the spaciousness of inner freedom. He was able to stand in Reality while responding compassionately to the distressing circumstances of his people. He did not deny the reality of what was happening in Tibet, nor the Reality of his inner freedom."

Michael is so aware, so clear in his outlook, here he notices with lucid accuracy the non-duality of another authentic person. Sharing such wisdom in his uniquely personal way, he leads the reader forward toward true spiritual liberation.

This book is a real manual to higher, freer living. It really works. It is an honor to riff a little coda in its wake.

Robert Thurman
Jey Tsong Khapa Professor of Buddhist Studies, Columbia University
President, Tibet House US
Author of *Why the Dalai Lama Matters* and many other books